The Other Side of Pain

the Other Side of Pain

KNOW YOUR POWER

overcoming childhood sexual abuse

VERONICA CRYSTAL YOUNG

Putnam & Smith Publishing Company

The Other Side of Pain
by
Veronica Crystal Young

Edited by CJ Schepers

Cover and Book Design by Michelle Radomski

Distributed by:
Putnam & Smith Publishing Company
15915 Ventura Boulevard, Suite 101
Encino, California 91436
www.putnamandsmithpublishing.com

Library of Congress Control Number: 2019907961

ISBN: 978-1-939986-26-9

Printed in the United States of America

To all survivors of childhood sexual abuse
who are ready to leave the past behind them,
reclaim their power, and create a new life
filled with happiness, abundance, and love.

"Nobody can protect anybody else from vileness.
Or from pain. All you can do is not let it break you in half
and keep on going until you get to the other side."

– Peter Straub

Table of Contents

Acknowledgments

"Gratitude unlocks the fullness of life. It turns what we have into enough, and more. It turns denial into acceptance, chaos to order, confusion to clarity. It can turn a meal into a feast, a house into a home, a stranger into a friend."

– Melody Beattie

I'm grateful and humbled by the many people and experiences I've encountered throughout my life. Learning how to navigate this journey of survival was at times exciting, challenging, and painful. My friends, family, and mentors have played a huge part in my continued growth and success as I live out the life I was meant to. I'm forever appreciative to all of them and my heart shines out the deepest thank-you to:

Mom, for her unconditional love and strength, even though she'd say she was not that strong (but she is).

My two older brothers, Ron and Wayne, for their diverse opinions, big-brotherly advice, and serving as an occasional mirror to my own pain, healing, and growth.

My younger brother Bert, for my beautiful, extended family, whom I learn from each and every day.

Cat Williford for her unending support, love, and friendship.

Eric Anderson, for his love, and gentle, grounding energy (as well as being an awesome guitar player and my beloved partner in co-creating our dreams!).

CJ Schepers, my editor and creative collaborator, for her dedication, intuitive clarity, and artistry in helping me craft what I wanted to say in an organized, powerful way.

The Goddesses, (you know who you are), for never failing to be there for me as well as each other.

My mentors, coaches, counselors, and clients, for guiding me to discover the true gold within and deeper levels of self-awareness that I never dreamt possible.

And lastly, God and Spirit, for being with me always and revealing the truth about who I really am and how much more I have to offer.

Introduction

Our Past Will No Longer Define Us

"On the night you were born, the moon smiled with such wonder, that the stars peeked in to see you, and the night wind whispered, 'Life will never be the same again.'"

– Nancy Tillman

WHAT THIS BOOK IS REALLY ABOUT

Our brains are powerful machines, that unfortunately, can also be rewired to believe false things about ourselves in the wake of tragedy and trauma. Childhood sexual abuse is one of the most traumatic experiences one can ever know. Our own identity and self-worth soon begin to shrink; what it means to feel loved and respected by others becomes tangled, distorted. Life becomes about keeping secrets, clinging to shame and guilt, carrying chronic emotional and psychic pain, feeling constant shadows of doubt, and a pattern of worry that imagines only the worst. Until we're willing to explore these negative, self-destructive thoughts, to reexamine the stories we tell ourselves about the past, to allow our feelings to swim to the surface where they can breathe, we will never be free to be us. Our true powers will sadly continue to evade us.

I've worked for many years to get to the other side of pain, to uncover and speak my truths, and to objectively, compassionately realize that what happened to me does not get to define me. Along the way, I have discovered a few key truths and tools to help me push through depression, thoughts of suicide, feeling alone and separate from others, the protective instinct to hide my own Light, and fear of showing my vulnerability as a human being who's survived childhood sexual abuse.

But one cannot have and experience love without risking vulnerability. As spiritual teacher and author Marianne Williamson writes so beautifully: "Our deepest fear is not that we are inadequate. Our deepest fear is that we are powerful beyond measure. It is our Light, not our Darkness, that most frightens us. We ask ourselves, who am I to be brilliant, gorgeous, talented and fabulous? Actually, who are you not to be? You are a child of God. Your playing small does not serve the world. There is nothing enlightening about shrinking so that other people won't feel insecure around you . . . As we let our own Light shine; we unconsciously give other people permission to do the same. As we're liberated from our own fear, our presence automatically liberates others."[1]

It's time, dear one, for you to remember who you really are, the Light that has always been yours. It's time for you to leave those negative thoughts and stifling, false stories behind. It's time to reclaim your confidence, brilliance, and the gifts with which you were born.

This is what this book is about. I'm here to hold your hand and heart, so together, we can repair your Psyche, reclaim your Life,

_____

1. Marianne Williamson, *Return to Love* (New York: HarperCollins, 1996), 190–191.

and reveal your inherent Powers. Throughout this book, you'll find true stories from other survivors, including myself, as well as exercises, meditations, and tips to help open up your awareness and consciousness, and to pull back the curtain on any chronic, negative thoughts and beliefs from the past that keep triggering you and, ultimately, mess with the fantastic potential of your present and future.

Yes, you do have the POWER to take back the reins of your life, dear ones, and to experience love, happiness, peace, success, and live out your special purpose on this planet in this body—now. It's never too late. Never.

So, let's get started.

How to Use This Book

Our Past Will No Longer Define Us

"On the night you were born, the moon smiled with such wonder, that the stars peeked in to see you, and the night wind whispered, 'Life will never be the same again.'"

– Nancy Tillman

Healing is never a linear A+B=C process.

At first, you may want to follow the chapters in order as you peel back the layers and gradually reveal what's been hiding beyond your own awareness. For that reason, I've organized this book into three parts: The Problem of Unresolved Pain, The Process of Transformation, and The Power That Is Yours. To get the most from this book, however, I urge you to start with the Introduction, then My Story and background, and you may likely find we have much in common. At the end of each chapter, I've also included exercises, tips, meditations, and affirmations to help you delve more deeply and quicken the journey—back to yourself.

Beyond that, as your passage to "the other side of pain" unfolds, you may feel pulled to read and absorb certain chapters over others, and want to scribble in the margins, highlight, and underline those parts that impact you most. There's no wrong way to use this book; this is *your* healing and *your* transformation.

This book was born out of pain and darkness (as all hero/heroine journeys are), so that you may find a way to shine your own Light brighter . . . and live more fully the life you deserve, need, and want.

The Problem of
Unresolved Pain

CHAPTER
1

Reclaim Your Powers

*"True belonging doesn't require us to change who we are;
it requires us to be who we are."*

– Brené Brown

As a little girl, I'd pedal my bike around our middle-class neighborhood, wearing a small, red blanket as my super-hero(ine) cape. That cape would flutter and fly in the breeze behind me . . . like wings on my shoulders! I felt free, invincible, happy. I just knew that someday—I'd grow up to live an amazing life. I could do and be anything I wanted! This was my world. My dreams. My choices. Like you, I was a born a grand and pure soul with some pretty amazing powers.

Of course, I couldn't shoot laser beams out of my eyes, control the weather, or shape-shift into an eagle (although hey, that would've been pretty cool). But I had other natural-born powers: traits, talents, skills, and quirks that just made me—me.

My early childhood memories are a bit foggy, but I do recall how much I loved pretending that I was a rock star, my little legs swaying to the music atop a large shelf ledge that was custom-built under the windows of our garage. I'd dance and sing on that imaginary stage, and sometimes my younger brother would join in, like Donny to my Marie. We were a hilarious sister-brother duo! One day during practice we realized, hey, our band needs a cool name. We scanned our surroundings, and the name Bandini stamped on a plastic bag caught my eye. And so, we became "The Bandinis!" Only later did we discover, ahem, that Bandini was a fertilizer company, and that the bag that first inspired us was full of manure compost!

Painting was another early passion of mine. Using acrylics, I painted a waterfall and forest scene on the backside of our garage door. Between music and painting, artistic expression was definitely my thing. It filled me with joy, love, and excitement. Being creative made me feel most alive. I felt like I could try anything artistic and be good at it. I was naturally self-confident and felt like I mattered to the world—that "I was somebody special!"

But once the abuse started that confidence, love, and excitement I was naturally born with quickly faded into the shadows. Soon, I began to believe that I wasn't really that good and shouldn't be putting myself "out there" at the center of attention. The shame and confusion shut me up for several years. It wasn't until I started high school that I attempted to reawaken my talents by taking choir and drama classes. My freshman year, I was frightened and anxious about that first talent show. But the fear of *not* doing it scared me more. Back then, Barbra Streisand was my idol and I'd chosen a popular song from the movie *A Star Is Born* to make my debut. I ended up winning the school contest, a big boost to my confidence. With my natural affinity for music rekindled, I started performing in musical theater.

The arts became my escape from the nightmare of home life. I could be me again (even if those wonder-filled moments were brief). But I also craved the attention to make me feel worthy of living.

It took years of therapy, self-help books, workshops, and life experiences to realize I didn't need outside validation to feel connected, to love and be loved, and to know my own worthiness. Slowly, I began to change my "reason" for performing. Instead of craving validation, the "why" behind my artistic expression transformed into wanting to make a positive difference in the world, to impact how people think of themselves and help them realize that they have the Power inside them to change. Today, I use my natural-born talents to directly influence others as a speaker and a life coach, and indirectly as an actress and singer.

Chances are, you remember feeling your own special powers, too, before you began to suffer the horrors of your abuse.

WHERE DO OUR POWERS GO?

For those of us who drew the unlucky straw of having to suffer at the hands of abuse, the birth-print that made us so unique may seem like it's gone. But I promise you: it's never gone. Trauma only forced those powerful parts of you into hiding, to a place of retreat where your inner child felt safer, less threatened. Trauma compelled you to adapt, to diminish parts of yourself in order to navigate the very real dangers that were impossible for you to cope with as a child. Like a python snake, trauma lunges out, coils around its victim, and attempts to suffocate the powerful soul you came forth as—until you can barely breathe.

But now you're a full-grown adult, right? And, your heart's still beating and you're still breathing. Which means you're still here— *and*—so are the magnificent powers you were born with.

I have a friend Amelia[2] who'd given up playing the piano, which she had once dearly loved, because her perpetrator had also loved the piano (but she didn't make the connection until much later in life). Even as an adult, she didn't know *why* she had suddenly turned her back on something that had given her so much joy, until she finally realized through the help of a therapist: she had unconsciously linked piano playing to the childhood sexual abuse. I helped guide her to work daily on replacing her old, false beliefs with new, healthy truths about herself, and eventually Amelia returned to her love for the piano.

"It takes Wonder Woman courage and Superman strength to heal the wounds of our abuse," Jeanne McElvaney, a veteran advocate in the field of healing childhood sexual abuse writes in her book *Healing Insights*. "Because it brings change . . . and we are inclined to hold on to the stability we created in the chaos of our past experiences. So, imagine more," she counsels. "Take small steps. Be guided by your personal truth and not the impressions left by the bad guys in your childhood story."

Another woman in her late-fifties told me how she longed to retrieve those parts of herself she once loved—before the abuse began at age ten. "For me," she explained, "it was my outgoing nature and strong confidence, my quirky humor, and fearless desire to be on stage. That's who I really was." Gradually, as the abuse continued, she lost that part of herself, became withdrawn

---

2. Not her real name.

and anxious, stricken with social anxiety disorder (which at the time, wasn't even on the medical radar), and suffered from PTSD. As a professional writer, she's worked hard to unlock the powers she once knew as a child, and through cognitive therapy and medication, delivered her first public book talk. "I was terrified, of course," she professed," but by the end of the talk, I knew I had freed and expressed a part of myself that was hidden for decades. So many people came up to me afterward to tell me how much I'd inspired them. That's when I realized I couldn't let the fear keep me silent anymore. It was a deeply spiritual milestone for me."

Like most survivors, you've hit those moments in your life where you've fallen into deep depression, despair, and disillusionment. You continued to believe the lies that family members and other trusted adults fed you in their attempt to hide their despicable crimes. No doubt, there have been chapters in the timeline of your being, your story on this planet, when you've been brought to your knees, literally (or let's be honest, curled up into a shivering fetal position) wondering, "Why me?" and "How can I find myself again?"

I can tell you from my own journey; it's at these darkest moments, that you also reach a turning point—a transformative place that holds the key to unlocking the superpowers you were born with. Powers inside you that are crying out to be heard and expressed once more.

I'm here to attest to you, dearest soul: it's on this very painful edge between the Dark and the Light, where you meet your truest self again, and can live the life you were meant to. It is never too late. Your inner child, the grand soul you were born as, is waiting to reemerge.

EXERCISES:
Your Superpowers Are Reflected in the Mirror of Your Stories

Here are two powerful exercises adopted from the book *Character Consciousness: Developing Self-Awareness Through Life Story Writing* with permission from the author Bernard Selling. In his fifty years of teaching adults how to rediscover themselves by writing (and rewriting) their own life stories, he found that most of his students, especially those who'd survived early trauma, failed to recognize their positive qualities and instead focused on negative aspects, such as hopelessness, victimization, laziness, and so on. "With a negative self-image at work, is it any wonder that our dreams do not become reality," he writes. One of his most effective methods is to instruct his students to write stories about themselves and look deeper into each story as if it were a mirror reflecting back the truth of who they were then—and are now. "A number of students/clients had experienced severe abuse or trauma in their childhood," he explains, "and so the process of reframing their view of themselves had to include knowing and reframing events that lay buried deep . . . "

Selling offers an example of a woman in her late forties, soft-spoken and somewhat removed. In each of her stories, however, she continued to see herself as "a victim—mute voiceless, devoid of will and energy." So, he suggested she write about the very first time she felt this way. Her next story was about being very young, roughly three years old, when her mother's boyfriend pulled her onto his lap and began to molest her. She still saw herself as a helpless victim. He then suggested she expand on the story, including what happened *afterward*. As she wrote more again, she recalled running out of the house and not coming back until the boyfriend was gone. "I asked her once more to look at herself in the mirror of her story," he explains, "and write what she saw reflected there." Finally, she began to see herself in a positive light. "I was spunky. Yes," she paused. "And, I took care of myself as best I could." By reframing her past experiences, she was able to gain awareness of her strengths and inner powers that had helped her survive. Until then, she'd never seen herself in such a positive light.

WRITING EXERCISE NO. 1

Take a memorable life event from the past, up to the age of twelve, and write a short story about it, making you the central character. Write it out in first person, in vivid detail, as if it's happening right now. Be sure to include the main character's inner thoughts and feelings (very important!). Don't get hung up on whether your writing is good enough. Just write.

Look at your first draft. Are you inside the story? Or outside the story? If you're outside the story and keeping that memory at arm's length, then you need to explore the event more deeply by putting yourself in the story as the *central character.*

Next, rewrite that same story, but with greater attention to detail, putting yourself centerstage. With this next version, your story's title may even change.

Now, compare both versions. Do you see a difference? Are your positive qualities emerging?

> **Keep rewriting the story until the positive qualities and true feelings of the main character (that's you) are revealed.**

You'll begin to see, perhaps for the first time, how your strengths and positive qualities emerged even during such traumatic events.

WRITING EXERCISE NO. 2

Jot down ten of your most significant character qualities that help you "see" that you're no longer a victim or weak, but instead, a brave, resilient person with kickass powers and positive character traits. Keep these close to help you remember.

1. _____

2. _____

3. _____

4. _____

5. _____

6. _____

7. _____

8. _____

9. _____

10. _____

CHAPTER
2

You Didn't Cause It

"You've been silenced long enough.
It was never your fault.
It's time to speak your truth,
take your place in the light, and start living."

– Mike Pistorino, adult survivor of child sexual abuse

Mom wasn't feeling well, again. She'd taken a few pills, the ones that knocked her out for the night. My brothers and I were watching one of our favorite TV shows, *All in the Family*. We, like millions of viewers back then, got a big kick out of the main character, a loud-mouth, narrow-minded patriarch called Archie Bunker (played by the late-great Carroll O'Connor) who'd spout off bigoted, socially rude comments and call his son-in-law "Meathead" (aka Rob Reiner). We thought the award-winning comedy was hilarious (although its controversial premise probably wouldn't survive long today).

After the show was over, it was our bedtime. I had my own room, the perfect little girl's retreat, my bed piled high with cute stuffed animals and a clean white dresser and mirror where I had carefully collected my most precious knickknacks over the years. I was getting ready for bed when Dad came in. "You know, your mother is asleep early every day because of you." I knew what he was talking about. Mom's depression had worsened after I had told her about Dad's "mistake," the first time he'd assaulted me.

This is how it begins. The perpetrator teaching and brainwashing the child that it was her or his fault. So, of course, I believed it.

My father's "teachings" and validations for his heinous actions included: leaving money on my dresser and then later calling me a prostitute for taking the money; warning me that my mother would have to go back to the hospital and that it was my fault she was there in the first place; and that since I took Mom away from him, it was my job to "take care" of him. I was the female, so I had to keep the family together and keep his sick secret. It was my responsibility. My fault. If only I was a better daughter, this never would have happened.

***I want you to really get this: You* never**
asked for or deserved what was done to you.

Let's be clear about where this notion of "it was my fault" in all forms comes from. You were told things about people, behaviors, or situations from those very same adults whom you trusted to have your best interest, to love and protect you. When they acted out from their own insecurities and mental sickness, in ways that harmed us, it was just too scary to believe we were that unsafe, that we were in real danger—within our own homes, neighborhoods, schools, and churches.

We rationalized that if we were only good enough, smart enough, lovable enough, then surely, they would love us and take care of us the way we wanted and needed. As we grew up in the world, this gave us a false sense of control over how others might treat us. Just be "good enough" (whatever that means), and "they" won't hurt us. Then, we'll hopefully be worthy of their love and respect.

For trauma survivors, another twisted piece of the puzzle is to realize that we, in fact, took care of the abuser's feelings over our own. I remember my father sitting on the edge of the bed, sobbing one night, saying he was sorry, like a repentant husband after hitting his wife. All I wanted was for the madness and pain to stop, to be "good enough or better" so *he would stop*. I clung to hope that maybe this would be the last time if only I could comfort him and say, "It's OK, Daddy, we'll be OK." He had programmed me to believe that "it" was my fault that somehow only *I* could "fix it"; a sick illusion that he counted on. It's no surprise that during most of my adult years, I often assumed too much control and responsibility, even for situations, people, and events that I did not own. I admit this has been a hard habit to break, in both my personal and professional life.

You may still feel the pull of "not enough" or "It's my fault." Working through these false feelings, however, will lead you to healing. You can't ignore them nor give into them. Awareness is one kickass power that will help you stop this kind of self-destructive thinking.

It's not your fault. You weren't responsible. You are more than enough, and you are worthy! Once you start to become aware that you were conditioned to believe otherwise, you will KNOW the Truth, you will feel your own Power, and you will remember how strong and amazing you are. I really want you to get this, feel this—and KNOW it!

I consider myself an always-evolving, spiritual person. I believe in the formidable power of self-awareness, acceptance, and forgiveness. I believe we can rise from the ashes of hell and reclaim the powers we were born with. And, I believe we can break the shackles of victimhood and emerge with an unshakable knowing and strength that roars out to the world, "This is who I am, and equally important, who I am not!"

In recent years, however, there's been a disturbing trend of victim-blaming among New Age circles—you see it in memes, read it in blogs, hear it on podcasts, and YouTube videos. I've personally used social media to share inspirational quotes of my own, such as "Be loyal to your future, not your past," and "The mind and raging thoughts can be a prison of our own making. Freedom is one choice away." These words remind us that *we do have a choice*—to be intentional with our thoughts, feelings, and actions—so we can reclaim our own life.

These ideas about how the Universe works mostly stem from the popular Law of Attraction principles that assert whatever you "think" you attract. Think positive thoughts, you manifest positive stuff. Think negative thoughts, you manifest negative stuff. And, I do believe that we have the power of choice to create what we want, and that yes, we can attract more of whatever we're focusing on the most. The problem, however, is when this principle is misused as a way to explain why bad things happen to good people (especially innocent children, or victims of sexual violence). Or, some may even believe that Karma came a calling to balance out the scales for the child's past-life transgressions; in other words, if the child was abused in this lifetime, he or she must've been the abuser in a previous incarnation. Living on the West Coast, I suspect that I'm exposed to these beliefs more than most.

Yes, we're all searching for answers to some of Life's hardest questions:

Why are innocent children abused, even murdered?

Why do terrible things happen to good people?

What's behind humanity's insane cycle of violence?

It's only natural to try and make sense of tragic events and horrific situations. Otherwise, it's like we're left to helplessly stand there and stare into a dark, bottomless pit—a place without any hope, reason, or protection; a place where we have absolutely zero control over our own lives, or the world around us. And that's a damn terrifying place.

But whenever I hear someone say that the reason a child (or anyone) is harmed is because they attracted it through their "vibration," I want to throw my phone across the room, punch a pillow, or set some blogger straight. That would mean that if anything bad were to happen to us, we'd be completely at fault. Think about it: our "vibration" would have to be 100 percent positive to avoid getting hurt. But seriously, can anyone honestly say that about themselves?

We're entitled to our opinions and beliefs, and I believe that the intention is well-meaning. Except, those who assert that the victim chose the abuse, are only dumping more pain and suffering on top of an already pretty big pile of it. No matter what shiny paper or eloquent words we wrap it in, the danger with these kinds of assertions is that they continue to shoot arrows straight into the victim's wounded heart. And, God forbid, that they even hold the abusers, the perpetrators, accountable for what they have done. This kind of "simplistic spirituality" also leaves no room in the equation of Life for deeply beautiful, healing human qualities, like empathy, compassion, and stepping up to help others through their darkest times.

Take it from me, victims struggle with their own self-worth. Anyone who's been abused decided a long time ago that it must've been his or her fault, or why else would someone like a parent, hurt them so badly? Anyone who's been victimized has been lugging around a frayed and tattered suitcase filled with guilt, shame, confusion, unworthiness, depression, grief, sorrow, and a lifetime of PTSD.

At the same time, I'm not denying there's plenty of truth in practicing a positive attitude. Numerous studies now show us that the power of positive thinking and visualizations does make life better: we feel happier and more relaxed, less stressed and anxious, develop stronger immune systems, and grow more confident and optimistic.[3]

But, did you or I create our own realities when we were sexually assaulted? Hell no. Even though, at the time, we took on the blame and wore it like an invisible, scarlet letter of shame. The truth is, there are victims. We once were victims

---

3. Mark Guidi, "5 Scientific Studies that Prove the Power of Positive Thinking," LinkedIn, March 22, 2016, https://www.linkedin.com/pulse/5-scientific-studies-prove-power-positive-thinking-mark-guidi

(and, as I say often throughout this book) there comes a time to drop the cloak of victimhood, so you can finally be free to create your own life, without all that baggage of the past telling you who "it" thinks you are and what you should feel and do today to feel accepted, loved, and worthy.

As Sandra Lee Dennis, author, teacher, and researcher on the interplay of depth psychology and spirituality, so eloquently puts it, "When you most need validation and support to get through the worst pain of your life, to be confronted with the well-meaning, but quasi-religious fervor of these insidious half-truths can be deeply demoralizing . . . this kind of advice feeds guilt and shame, inhibits grieving, encourages grandiosity and can drive you to be alone to shield your vulnerability."

It was *not* your fault. You did not attract it. For your sake and others, please reject such simplistic ideas. Not only are they harmful and wrong, they're just downright cruel. DO take responsibility for your choices and actions today, however, because the present is exactly where your power awaits.

THE THING ABOUT SEXUAL ABUSE & THE BODY'S RESPONSE

One of the biggest hurdles I think survivors of sexual abuse have to overcome are feelings of shame, guilt, and fault. Especially if that abuse occurred during their prepubescent years. The shame of being judged with a comment like "you should have known better at your age;" the shame of their bodies betraying them because of a normal, physiological response (utterly confusing to a child or teen); and the shame that somehow, because they kept silent, they must have contributed to the abuse.

I remember when I first confessed to my therapist, there were times in my early teens, when the natural excitement after a date or movie with a boy had me looking for that shadow on my door. Even writing this today I think, "What am I doing! People will not understand." But the reality is, the human body is built for arousal. If you're still in doubt, I urge you to watch the TED Talk "The Truth About Unwanted Arousal"[4] by sex educator Emily Nagoski (2018). She explains, " . . . If we can find our way through all of the messy feelings, I believe we will find our way to the light of compassion for that child, whose relationship with her body was damaged by an adult whose job it was to protect it." Nagoski continues: "And we'll find hope that there was a trustworthy adult, who could say, 'Genital response just means it was a sex-related stimulus; doesn't mean it was wanted or liked, certainly doesn't mean it was consented to.'"

I want others who have felt similar shame and guilt to know that they're not alone and that our bodies are built this way. It wasn't sex; it was sexual abuse! I want them to know that keeping the abuse a secret and feeling the horrified confusion of it all is what drove them to internalize the shame, to try and make sense of the trauma in the first place. It's common to invent stories that we were worthless, unlovable, or just plain bad. Your brain gets rewired from the trauma, and that's ALSO *not* your fault.

If the abuse happened during your prepubescent years, and the abuser was a family member or close friend, not only was your sexuality deeply affected in a traumatic way, but so was your sense of security, trust, and love. This explains why those who've survived sexual abuse (and other abuses), fall into destructive behaviors and patterns, and feelings of low self-worth.

---

4. Emily Nagoski, "The Truth About Unwanted Arousal," TED Talk, https://www.ted.com/talks/emily_nagoski_the_truth_about_unwanted_arousal/transcript?language=en (accessed April 2019).

To heal fully, I had to accept that I had zero control over my body's normal reactions. So, F the shame. Be real and know in your bones that you didn't cause this, on any level. It's paramount to your healing, your inner peace, and creating your own powerful, loving life.

AFFIRMATIONS TO REMIND YOU:

We hear the words and they touch something deep inside us that knows—this is Truth. But then, the words fade. I urge you to say these affirmations often (choose the ones that resonate most clearly for you). Or, jot down some of your own. I've written powerful affirmations on Post-it notes, then placed them in my office, and around the house. You can even put them in your phone and set them up as alerts or reminders. These affirmations are your compass to keep you from getting lost again, or ever losing sight of how amazing you are.

- *I never asked for or deserved the abuse.*
- *I am responsible for my choices moving forward as an adult.*
- *I am growing more aware that my childhood pain left me with false beliefs and lies about myself.*
- *I am lovable and worthy and need validation from no one.*
- *I am courageous and powerful.*
- *Everything I choose today impacts my future. My choices are powerful.*
- *I am no longer a victim. I am the hero(ine) of my life.*

CHAPTER
3

Your Inner Critic & Its False Beliefs

"When patterns are broken, new worlds emerge."

– Tuli Kupferberg

The mind is a beautiful thing. Unfortunately, it can also be our worst enemy. We have up to 60,000 thoughts per day, and *80 percent of those are negative,* with the majority being the same thoughts as the day before, according to the National Science Foundation. That's a whole lot of negativity buzzing around in our brains. Psychologists call this phenomenon "automatic negative thoughts" or ANTs. Yep, there are thousands of ANTs scurrying around in our psyches with nothing much constructive to offer us, except poop on our parade. Like Buddha wisely said, "Your worst enemy cannot harm you as much as your own thoughts, unguarded."

Never ever assume negative thoughts are real, and always question and challenge them, says Dr. Daniel G. Amen, a neuropsychiatrist and *New York Times* bestselling author. In *Change*

Your Brain, Change Your Life, he urges people to practice turning any ANT (Automatic Negative Thought) into a PAT (Positive & Affirming Thought). "When a negative thought goes unchallenged, your mind believes it and your body reacts to it," Amen asserts. "ANTs have an illogical logic. By bringing them into the open and examining them on a conscious level, you can see for yourself how little sense it really makes to think these kinds of things to yourself."

So, we humans are predisposed to think far more negatively than positively. But the encouraging news is *we can change that.* Negative thinking is nothing more than a habit—a pattern we can interrupt, so a new mind can emerge.

> **For those of us who've experienced childhood trauma, those negative, repetitive thoughts come even faster, stronger. It's the voice of a highly critical parent, teacher, family member or adult telling us we can't do anything right, or that we're worthless, ugly, stupid, etc.**

Along the way, we bought into it: unconsciously absorbing and believing in the bullhorn of that voice. But it has never served us.

The real trouble with the inner critic is that we believe these thoughts are true.

NAME IT TO TAME IT

Strong emotions are a gift and a curse. If a reckless driver cuts you off on the freeway, and almost causes you to crash, you're likely to feel some pretty intense emotions (feel free to fill in the blank here). But if you're having a rage-filled response because you "think" your colleague just suggested you were lazy, well then, you've got a problem. You need to find a way to calm that beast down. Not ignore it. But step back and reduce the steam between your ears, so that the triggers of your abusive past aren't the ones running the show.

A friend once shared with me how her therapist taught her an ingenious tip on how to handle any tough, recurring intense emotional situation or subject (e.g., a health problem, a difficult relative, an addiction, money stress, and so on). He told her simply, "name it to tame it," a phrase and method invented by author and psychiatrist Dr. Daniel Siegel. Give it some kind of innocuous name that lightens the feeling around the problem or worry. This doesn't mean you're ignoring or denying the issue, or chronic thought. It actually means you're learning to *reframe* how you think and talk about it, so "it" will stop depleting your peace of mind and sucking all the beauty and joy from your life. Well, as the proverb goes, necessity *is* the mother of invention, and I've been doing this long before I'd heard about Dr. Siegel's "name it to tame it" method.

My "inner critic" can be so strong at times, so debilitating, that I had to name it to tame it. You have an inner critic, too. You know that voice. The one that's eager to tell you everything that's wrong with you, and why you can't possibly be, have, or do what you want. "I'm too old" ... "too young" ... "I'm weak" ... "I'm a loser" ... "I should've known better" ... "Why didn't I?" ... "Why can't I get my act together?" ... "I'll never be good enough." The problem with the inner critic is that it never motivates or inspires us. In fact, it does exactly the opposite. Makes us feel defeated. Ashamed. Anxious. Makes us want to give up. The inner critic's intensity is different for everyone. Allow me to introduce you to mine. Meet "Fred in the Head."

Giving my inner critic a name helps me have a dialogue with him, so I don't fall for such dismal, destructive self-talk. It helps me keep my positive, rational voice in charge. This is an extremely effective technique I use whenever I'm trying to decipher where the "can'ts" and "shoulds," the "fears and regrets" are really coming from. Whenever Fred in the Head pipes in, I ask my inner critic, "Why do you believe that?" and then wait for his response. Then, I ask, "Well, where did that come from? Where did you get *that* idea?" It's an effective method of getting to what's underneath my negative thoughts and false beliefs. It swiftly reveals the true feelings hiding underneath my defeatist beliefs. That way, I can examine the vulnerability and fear that's really doing the talking, the true emotion that triggered me in the first place. It stops Fred in the Head in his tracks and quiets those abusive refrains that only keep me paralyzed and stuck.

Negative self-talk is not reality-based (unless you're evaluating whether something is good for you or not, which is critical thinking, and not to be confused with negative thinking).[5] I'm sure you've heard that a belief is only a thought that you've repeated enough times in your mind that it becomes a belief. Your negative thoughts and beliefs become a habitual way of trying to make sense of the pain you've experienced. They're not real, and they're not serving you.

Once you become aware that your inner critic's voice is negative thinking (not constructive thinking), then you can

---

5. Critical thinking involves looking at a problem or issue with healthy skepticism, searching for the truth, researching, and reflecting in a clear, rational, open-minded way, so you end up making things better, not worse. It's not the same as that inner critical voice that only tears you down.

start to practice a new habit of positive, more rational thinking that puts *you in charge of your own life.* You'll start to question how correct or wise that inner-critic voice really is before you make any decision, and before you allow it to drag you into a pointless pit of depression, self-pity, and despair.

It isn't easy to stay positive when negativity surrounds you. You have to be in enough pain, to be tired of where your life is at and where it's going, to really go for it! It won't happen overnight; in fact, negative thinking never stops because everyone's thoughts are nonstop.

> *Once you become aware of those thoughts that are limiting your potential, however, and once you see the lies for what they are, you begin to think new, empowering thoughts—even when you're dealing with life's most grueling circumstances.*

EXERCISE:
Name & Challenge Your Inner Critic

What comes up as Fred in *your* Head? That critical voice that brings up all the excuses and reasons you can't do or have the life you want? Take a few minutes to jot down some names that come to mind, and then choose the one that make you feel instantly lighter (it may even make you smile or laugh out loud). It could be "Cousin It," or "Negative Nelly" or "Fraidy Brady." Well, you get the idea. The point is to finally let go of giving too much attention to your inner critic and all its chronic worries. This exercise can be the beginning of a new directional shift and powerful change for you, from the inside-out. For example:

Valerie is a single, working mother who's gained 10 pounds in the last year. Her demanding job has cut into her exercise time, and the stress is causing her to eat more and spike her cortisol levels. She goes shopping and tries on her usual size. Nothing fits. Her inner critic kicks in: "God, I'm so fat. I hate my body. What if I get fatter? I'm so ugly."

What is Valerie really afraid of? She asks her inner critic, who responds, "I'm afraid you'll never meet a man and fall in love again if you can't be your smaller size."

What is she really feeling vulnerable about? Valerie is feeling a deep loss for the body she used to have. She feels a loss of control over her life. She's afraid she'll always be alone.

What Valerie says next to her inner critic goes something like this, "I get that you want to protect me. I appreciate it. But I'm also proud of the work that I do, and that I'm a great mom, loving daughter, fun friend, and amazing woman. And, I'm still beautiful and very spunky. If I really want to lose some weight, I'll find a way."

Anytime your inner critical voice pipes up, ask yourself:

- Is this thought real?
- Is this thought helping me?
- Is this thought making my life any better?
- What if I didn't have this thought at all anymore?

The next time you hear an inner-critic thought, write it down *immediately*—in the second person (saying "You," instead of "I"), such as, "You're so lazy," "You'll never get what you want," "You always screw things up," etc. Whatever your inner critic is blathering on about. Now, how does that negative thought make you *feel?* Really dive into that feeling.

Then tell your inner critic that you get why and where this is coming from—to protect you. But let your inner critic know (and this is crucial): "Your negative feedback isn't helping me. I'm not ugly, or bad, or a failure. I need you to speak to me with more compassion so I can do something constructive about how I'm feeling or else accept the way it is and be freakin' happy. So, thanks for trying buddy, but no thanks."

CHAPTER
4

Release Regrets

"Rolling in the muck in not the best way of getting clean."

– Aldous Huxley

Here's the crazy thing about regret. We'll always have regrets; it's part of being human. But the tricky thing about regret is even *if* we could travel back in time and relive those moments; if we were magically offered the opportunity to make different choices, to take a different path, to get a metaphysical do-over—we have no way of knowing if the outcome would've turned out differently! And people like us who've survived trauma and abuse tend to hold onto regret more than most. *If only things had been different*, we wonder. If only, if only, if only . . .

Then, there are some regrets that even if we could erase them, would as a consequence, also erase those exact moments and events that made us everything we are today. With all our awesome traits and talents, flaws and quirks, we are one beautiful, limited edition. Consider Edward Lorenz's physics/chaos theory, the phenomenon called the "butterfly effect," where even the smallest changes give rise to significant, far-reaching outcomes. Psychologically and spiritually, we'd end up erasing something that was necessary for us to learn and grow from (not only us, but also the impact it had on others we knew, and the people they knew, and on and on as the ripples of our lives interconnect). Every choice we make has an impact.

For example, let's say you could go back and avoid that blind date or turn down that job offer that wasn't what you wanted? Let's say that blind date led to marriage and a child, but then later turned into a soul-sucking divorce. Let's say you regret ever meeting him, went back in time, and skipped that first date, never falling in love in the first place. Where would your child be then? Never born. Or, you might have met and fell in love with someone else who caused you even greater pain.

Perhaps that job you hated had a silver lining: it led you to connect with others, make new friends, and evolve your skills and build relevant experience so that you eventually landed the job of your dreams. Or, maybe the pain of that miserable job was enough to kick you in the ass, so you'd make a pivotal career change, or go back to school, or pursue work you loved.

Perhaps the pain of abuse made you stronger and more determined to do whatever it took to live a meaningful life and shine the Light that is YOU. To find your true self and create your own happiness, regardless of any and all obstacles because you knew deep down that you could do it and would do it, day by day, step by step, mile by mile.

You see: every ripple in your life, big or small, has a force of its own.

Regret is an utterly draining, negative emotion because it's attached to the past, not the present. Regret always lives in the past; you can never regret something that's happened in the future. Even if you regret something that happened five minutes ago, as soon as you feel it, the time has passed. No amount of regret can change what's happened. Nor, can you assume you had control over those regrets in the first place. There are choices we've willingly made. And then there are choices that others made—without our consent. So, how could you ever regret something you had zero control over?

I've had some deep regrets.

For example, for years, I found it difficult to find the right partner, so finding my man later in life than most is one regret. And yet, I've come to understand: What if I had married the wrong person? Or married him *too soon?* Before I was ready?

Life is a mystery, and often, we must trust the reason.

I always wanted children and a loving family to call my own. As a survivor of sexual abuse, even though I had worked for years on healing my own emotional, physical, and spiritual pain, I still believed that I lacked the fortitude and merit to raise my own kids. *How could I ever bring a child into such a cruel, messed-up world, especially when all the statistics and evidence insisted there was a high chance that the cycle repeats for the next generation?* I held onto a deep fear of perpetuating that. Of course, I see now that this was a story, I'd made up out of fear.

I've never been one to think that a woman needs motherhood to feel fulfilled, but I do understand and respect why others feel that way. At the same time, I now see that raising a child would have brought me more joy and love, personal growth and a fresh perspective on life. It's something I regretted, and yet, I had to fully feel it—and then release that regret. True, I don't have children of my own, but today I can reach out to children and adults and fight for their right to speak out about past pain and how it affects them today. I get to live my purpose as a champion for the unconditional love, happiness, and healing they so deeply deserve.

> *Regret is neither helpful nor healthy. It makes us crazy! It's like that tiny crumb or spot of dust that has a record needle stuck, playing the same part of the song, over and over and over—and never getting past it.*

For God's sake, move that frickin' needle! Clean out that debris, no matter how small it is—'cuz baby, that loop ain't gonna fix itself.

Regret appears whenever we feel sadness, shame, embarrassment, depression, guilt—and we ache for a different outcome. But ruminating and wishing for things to be different is like living on a totally different planet. The reality is, if something is done, it's done. No amount of regret will change that. Of course, that doesn't mean you shouldn't take the time to reflect and see what there is to learn from the regret. Hey, honestly, it's necessary to feel the hurt and pain. Especially if it fuels you to get out of your wallowing and do something about it. I know it has me.

I confess, now and then, I still catch myself sinking back in the quicksand of regret. Even with all my years of awareness and training around it, boy, does it sneak up on me! But once I've acknowledged it, I then pledge to myself: *Next time, make better choices, Veronica. Be proactive and give yourself permission to put yourself first.* Or, *don't dismiss your intuition.* Then I fully release the regret, which always includes forgiving myself—and others.

For instance, whenever I'm working crazy long hours at the hospital, I can slip into regret about being short-tempered or cranky with others. Usually, once I'm aware of this and reflect on it, I see that I'm not giving my creativity and personal life enough energy, passion, and focus. And, that's when I realize: *Hey, Veronica, it's time to **make time** . . .* to practice singing that song, writing that chapter, or planning a cool getaway with my (very understanding) man.

As I mature and evolve, I'm less prone to feeling regret; I have the wisdom to realize that when I make a mistake, or what I feel is a mistake, it's something I needed to experience to keep growing and blooming. I also know that I need to release it for my own well-being and others. The past is past us. Reflect and then take any action to address it (if it is indeed your regret to own in the first place). When you begin to do this with a regret, you'll not only become a happier, healthier, wiser person—but you'll also show others how to do the same.

Life is a wonderful journey. Don't pack
your suitcase with the dirty laundry of regret.

TIPS:
How to Release Regret

We all have regrets. The important thing is not to roll around in the mud, as Huxley put it. Whenever you feel yourself wallowing in regret, do these five steps *immediately* to pull yourself out of it. It doesn't guarantee that everything will turn out the way you want it to. After all, you can only control what you say or do—not others.

But once you step into your power and own it, by learning from regret, you'll start to feel better about your choices and behavior. In turn, this new habit around regret will diminish the pain, and even eliminate having a regret in the first place.

1. First, allow yourself to fully feel and reflect on the regret. Sometimes it helps to put a time limit on this reflecting period (no more than 10 minutes), especially if the pain feels too overwhelming. Journaling, putting your thoughts on paper will help you release your regret.

2. When reflecting, ask yourself, "What can I learn from this?" Instead of taking on the role of victim, steeping in self-pity, or beating yourself up for some negative behavior, ask yourself, "How I can grow and learn from this experience?" "What can I learn about myself and others?"

3. If possible, take some action to heal or resolve the situation with others (this may not be an option; it depends on the regret).

4. Consider how you might react differently in the future to influence the outcome and practice what you'd say or do in a similar situation—without any judgment. Remember, this is the school of Life, and we only learn through experience, right?

5. Accept it, forgive yourself and others, and then move on. Say to yourself, *next!* Believe me, there will always be another situation that causes you regret, which means a fresh opportunity to respond or approach the situation differently.

CHAPTER 5

Summon the Courage

*"It takes courage to grow up
and become who you really are."*

– E.E. Cummings

Courage. The word itself conjures up searing images in our collective human psyche. Visions of soldiers charging into battle to face pain, defeat, and even death . . . a man fighting cancer and undergoing debilitating treatments, his days ahead of him shaky, unknown . . . the nightmare of an anxious child, seeing her father's shadow cast upon the bedroom door, and praying that this time, he leaves her the hell alone.

*Courage is never easy. I've learned the hard
way (like all life/soul lessons) that courage
is a choice we make in the moment—
moment to moment—for the rest of our lives.*

But as children, we were far too vulnerable, too defenseless, physically *and* emotionally, to stand up for what was right and protect ourselves. For most of us, courage meant facing an assault from the person we trusted most, so we could survive another day.

Today, as an adult, however, courage now calls on us to summon it in a different way: to create the life we really want and deserve. It's the stuff that heroes and heroines are made of. That's why archetypal stories about super powered beings (think Superman, Wonder Woman, Batman, etc.) resonate so deeply within us. Because these iconic characters were created to literally reach into our hearts, minds, and souls—daring us to reawaken the superpowers we were born with.

Yes, the call to courage is *real*.

In today's frenetic, overly-plugged-in world in which technology is replacing human connection; where jobs seem sparser and tempers higher; and where psychological, physical, and spiritual neglect continues to generate more self-doubt, pain, and fear—we've never needed the "higher" vibration of courage more than now. Yes, I said "vibration." Others may define courage as a quality, emotion, or virtue. But ultimately, at its core, it's a vibration. An energy. Pure, yet, not-so-simple, I admit.

That's because there are other "lower" vibrations that constantly resist and challenge the power of courage, such as cowardice, apathy, and conformity (yes, going with the majority "yeas" in the room, or blindly following your tribe's unspoken agreements—so you can play it safe and avoid ruffling any human feathers—even when you *know* that it hurts the greater good, and doesn't reflect who you truly are). These lower vibrations temporarily make you feel safe and comfortable. But sadly, they also keep you in a holding pattern: playing it small, and ultimately, living as a specter of your true self. Then one day, you look in the mirror, and realize: *This is not the magnificent person I was born to be!* I've lost myself— all in the name of wanting to belong.

Courage is about summoning the nerve to speak up and act on your dreams. To tell your truth especially in the face of your fears (and the fears of others). Fears of being criticized, rejected, unloved. It's not easy. Being courageous is having the guts to place yourself in situations that are hard and challenging, out of your comfort zone, and frankly, will feel risky, or at least "perceived" as risky. Especially as survivors of traumatic abuse, we're often swayed by our expectations of what might happen, or what others will think of us.

But here's the truth: The past is behind you. It's never your future or your fate, unless you think it is. Right now, your life today, is the only true time you have left.

Notice how I didn't say fear was the opposite of courage? Fear was never meant to be defined that way (despite what a dictionary or thesaurus tells you). Honestly, think about it: how could there ever be such a thing as courage without the vibration of fear, which is actually the fuse that lights the act of courage? As humorist and columnist Franklin P. Jones aptly put it, "Bravery is being the only one who knows you're afraid."

"This 4th of July holds special meaning for me," I wrote in my journal several years back. "We all know what courage our forefathers needed to forge an entirely new country. But this year, I've witnessed the power of courage in some of my closest friends and family members, and I, too, have had to muster up a big, healthy dose of it."

You see, a mother and close friend of mine had to face some devastating news about her own family. The father was soon returning home after an extended business trip, and the younger sister confided to her older sister that she was petrified at the thought of seeing him. Clearly, something was wrong here, and not to be ignored. After hours of questioning and tough, tearful conversations, my friend called me around midnight. Once the truth came out—that he'd been sexually abusing his own daughter—the mother divorced him, and the girls are now safe again. I couldn't help but think how courageous that little girl was for speaking up and seeking help. I found myself grappling with my own abuse, and how I stayed silent, terrified that if I *ever* told anyone, it would be *my fault* for breaking up the family. And, I couldn't help but wonder how that might have altered the course of my life, if only I'd spoken up. And yet, I'm who I am today because of, and despite the abuse.

What happened to me in the past will always be a part of me, and yet, it doesn't get to define me!

Even though you may literally shake at the thought of it, if you truly want to change your life for the better, it's time to answer the call to courage. To speak up and be heard. To face a challenging goal or situation. To throw down the gauntlet and go for it! To make choices from your own heart, not the expectations of others. I'm talking about the courage to be vulnerable and real. The courage to be 1,000 percent—*you*. Your heart will know it, so trust it. I've learned to, and so will you. Even though you can't see that far ahead, or around the next corner.

As you walk your own path to healing, you'll
realize how much of yourself was lost or
hidden in those earlier years; yet, I promise
you—you'll also feel optimistic and eager
to know that you're finding your way back—to you.

In truth, you've already answered the call to courage because
. . . you're still here and reading this now. Question is, what will
you do next?

THE "UNCOMFORTABLE" COMFORT ZONE

As a transformation and leadership coach, I understand all too
well how our past emotional triggers are often roadblocks to our
success as adults, especially whenever we need to summon the
courage to take action outside our comfort zone. The comfort
zone is that place in life that we've grown too comfortable with—
even though it makes us feel unfulfilled and uncomfortable with
ourselves—we're afraid to tiptoe outside of what we've been used
to. Whenever we find ourselves in unfamiliar territory, it can feel
very threatening to try something different and new. It can make
us feel anxious and vulnerable.

The problem is: Always living inside your comfort zone doesn't
allow you to experience new, exciting people, places, and things.
You stagnate, even though you may desperately want (and need)
some change and growth. Those old childhood feelings can set off
your anxiety, up the ante on your need for outside approval, shrink
your confidence, and increase that crummy (but false) feeling of
unworthiness. Usually, this is because you've been telling yourself
these false stories that only diminish who you really are and what
you can really handle. Like a turtle, you may retreat into the

comfort of your "uncomfortable" shell, which ultimately, makes you feel even more alone and isolated, unfilled and invisible, and stuck. You become like the "frog in the boiling water"—the parable of a frog sitting in a pot of tepid water, never realizing the danger he's in as the water is brought to a very slow boil. Little by little, the temperature continues to rise, until eventually, the poor thing cooks to death (when all the frog had to do was hop the hell out of there!).

Post-traumatic stress can keep us in a cycle of avoidance—to the point where we numb out or disconnect from our true feelings as a way to temporarily deal with any uncomfortable situations. Rationally, we know that whatever happened wasn't our fault, and yet, we still have those nagging, negative feelings that hold us back. It's not enough to "know" what's happening—we have to "feel" that we deserve more and can handle it. And, we can only get there by trying, through experience.

Of course, taking risks and pushing past your comfort zone won't guarantee you'll get what you want every time. You may, you may not. But if you never try, you'll never know or grow. Ever. Truth is, there's no easy, risk-free path to success. But there are invaluable lessons and deeply personal levels of growth along the way, and you will reap fantastic rewards, I promise. Look, we've all had failures, setbacks, and disappointments. But if you practice reframing those experiences, you'll soon see that they helped you grow as a person, especially if you learned from your mistakes, owned them, and also realized—that some circumstances were simply out of your control. You did the best you could with the information you had. Period.

Pushing outside that comfort zone takes courage, believe me. You will feel fear, guaranteed. But that's *exactly* why you must begin to throw down the gauntlet and refuse to let fear and past trauma keep running your life.

It's in the self-awareness, beyond the ego,
that we begin to clearly see that our
thoughts about ourselves are only that—thoughts
that are stopping us from expressing our full power.

Sadly, for many people, they won't take the action they need to until the pain of a current situation becomes unbearable. Don't waste time waiting for *that to happen.* Look at your future self and begin to lean into and visualize the life you know you want. *What brings you joy and lights you up? Who do you want to share your life with? Aren't you ready to finally be who you are?*

EXERCISE:
The Wheel of Courage

It takes courage to look at our lives with complete honesty so we can change course and make our way back to us. For me, one of those pivotal moments was when I realized I had married a man who was very controlling, like my father. Once I saw the truth of our relationship, I had to summon the courage to take care of and protect myself and divorce him. It may sound strange, but I thank him for giving me the opportunity to grow and rediscover my true self. Even though at the time, it was confronting to admit that I had made a mistake. I was raised Catholic, so getting married at age nineteen and divorcing at twenty-one certainly hurt my sense of belonging to the church.

"The Wheel of Courage" below is meant to inspire and help you look deeper. Give yourself some quiet space and time to reflect on each of these areas of your life, each spoke of the wheel, and write down your most honest, heart-centered answers. You may want to revisit The Wheel of Courage every few months, as everything in life does constantly change.

1. What would I have to give up or change to heal this part of my life?
2. What might change and heal as a result of me summoning the courage to speak up, to take charge, and finally own my own choices in creating my new, amazing life?

THE WHEEL OF COURAGE

Making Conscious Changes and Owning Your Choices Takes Both Courage and Action

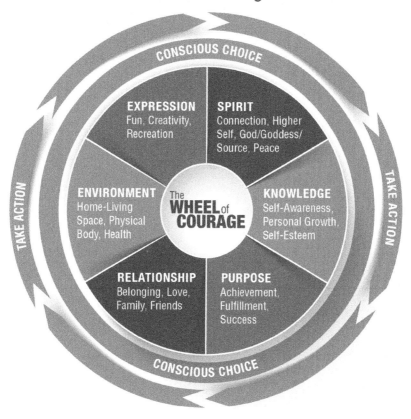

CHAPTER
6

The Family You Had vs. The Family You Create

"Refuse to inherit dysfunction. Learn new ways
of living instead of repeating what you lived through."

– Thema Bryant-Davis

Family. Good or bad, they played critical roles in our development. Either wittingly or unwittingly, our families passed onto the next generation (us) what they learned from their own upbringing. The family who raised you, whether you like it or not, shaped your earliest views of yourself and others, and Life, in general.

Dysfunctional families are called that because they don't "function" properly. There is betrayal, pain, neglect, and shame all mixed with fear, denial, manipulation, and yes, love. Our family is where we learn to communicate, express our feelings, respect others and ourselves, and feel a true sense of belonging and love.

Everyone's family dynamic is different, and the trauma each of us has experienced, along with some serious aftereffects, are complex. There are emotional, physical, and spiritual scars we will always bear, no matter how old and wise we become. Yet, if we're determined to live as the beautiful beings we once were— and stop the cycle of abuse forever—we must work on healing our deepest wounds. We must find a way back to us.

Those of us who've survived terrible childhood trauma come from all sorts of backgrounds. Blue-collar, white-collar. Barely educated, highly educated. Poor and middle-class, upper-class and jet setters. Married birth parents. A birth parent and stepparent. Adopted parents. Single mother, single father. Raised by other relatives like grandparents, aunts, and uncles. Only child, middle child, oldest child. Regardless of what your connection to the family that raised you is like today; those family bonds are as strong as bands of iron. And, for those of us who grew up in dysfunctional, abusive homes, that is *not* a good or healthy thing.

In the U.S. alone, one out of three girls and one out of five boys will be sexually abused before the age of eighteen, according to childtrauma.org. And, it's rarely a stranger who commits the crime, but someone inside the family, or another trusted adult.[6]

Sometimes, as survivors of abuse, we have to let go of certain family members and create our own family (including a circle of supportive, loyal friends).

Despite the famous adage, blood isn't always thicker than water.

A friend of mine, Carrie, now in her sixties, recalls the moment she realized she had to cut off what was left of the family that had

---

6. Susanne Babbel MFT, PhD, "Trauma: Childhood Sexual Abuse: Sexual abuse can lead to Post Traumatic Stress Disorder (PTSD)," *Psychology Today*, March 12, 2013.

raised her. Her own mother and stepfather had beaten and verbally abused her since she was nine. Then, at age fifteen, her birth mother died. Her stepfather fell into a bottle of booze to numb his grief, and continued the abuse as before, with an added twist: molestation. At eighteen, she left home.

By age twenty-two, Carrie was a divorced, single mom of two little girls, trying her damnedest to pretend she still had some kind of normal family. She explained. "My younger half-brother was in deep denial about what had happened to me all those years; he just wanted me to stay in the family and forget about it."

One day, her stepfather called, saying he wanted to see her and the kids. He'd already been drinking by the time they arrived, and after about an hour or so, his eyes turned dark, his face wild. "I knew that look," she sighed heavily. "I'd seen it too many times. I knew what was coming." Even though he'd beaten her so many times as a child and teenager, Carrie never dreamt he'd do it to her as a grown woman, and in front of her children, no less. "I started crying; I was so confused. One minute he was fine, and then the next . . ." her voice trailed off.

Suddenly, he reached out and grabbed Carrie's arms, shaking her and screaming with rage. "In that moment, all I could think about were my kids, they were two and three years old. I looked down and saw their eyes wide with fear, and my oldest daughter was trembling. I managed to pull myself away from him, grab both girls, and bust through that door. My stepfather actually chased me out into the yard, still screaming. I couldn't get into my car fast enough. My hands were shaking so badly, I'm surprised I could hold onto the steering wheel."

A few blocks away, she pulled over and tried to calm herself down. Then she drove straight home and called a mental health line. "That was my first talk with a therapist, and I vowed never again to expose myself or my children to that kind of craziness." Her decision wasn't without loss, however, because her brother stopped talking to her for many years. He was so angry that she'd left the "family."

"We finally started talking again about five years ago," she said, softly. "It took decades before we reconnected. But I did what was right for my own family. I didn't want my girls to grow up thinking that abuse and violence was 'normal' family stuff."

Carrie's story reminded me how hard it is to go through life wishing and praying for something better from the family that raised you or hoping that someday the person who abused you might change.

When I was going through therapy and it came time to confront my father, I couldn't believe how scared I was. Even at twenty-eight, he still had a hold on me. I remember driving down the freeway and spotting his car. When I glanced over and saw him, I sped up so fast, hoping he wouldn't see me. My heart was racing as fast as my car, and I couldn't believe how powerfully negative and terrifying the trigger was. It had been at least six years since I'd last seen him.

It would take another seven years before I made the decision to meet with him. There were two reasons. First, I wanted to hear him acknowledge the fact that he'd assaulted me, repeatedly, and that it was his fault. Second, I wanted to hear him say he was sorry and mean it. I guess the apology was really the most powerful part for me, because in my mind, maybe if he was truly sorry, then maybe he did love me after all. Maybe he wanted to be a good father, but his demons of the past took over. Maybe he had little self-control, but still, I wanted him to take responsibility for *that.*

When we did meet, it was a huge cathartic release of shame and blame for me, and validation of the abuse. (I write more about this encounter in the chapter "Forgiveness Is for You.")

*When we realize that the family that raised us is too
toxic to continue a relationship with,
we're faced with a difficult choice: to stay—or to go.*

I'm lucky that I found a life partner who helps me remember who I really am and supports my soul's purpose. Together, we've created a strong, healthy family, including a close group of trusted friends. If you have children, they will help you reevaluate your own life, and how you see the world. Tell them as often as possible, how much you love and care about them Love them and appreciate them with all your heart, for despite the trying times (and there'll be plenty!), the family you create become your anchors to your new life . . . and to who you really are.

MY OWN PARENTS

As Father's Day came around again, I found myself wanting to write about that day's subject—dads. We all have one: some of us knew our father, some of us didn't. If you were raised by your father, I'll bet that when you were little, yours seemed larger than life. This can be a positive or a negative, depending on who he was for you. As children, we expect and trust our fathers to protect and provide for us.

We get a lot from our parents. How relationships work, and how they don't. How to trust, or not trust. How to love, how to hate. Being a parent is a huge responsibility, actually one of the biggest, most important responsibilities in a person's life. Some people are meant to be parents, some not. No matter which type of parent you think you are or will become (or choose not to ever take on that role), know that you have a great impact on the little ones of this world, especially your own.

Dad was very dedicated to us when we were young. He worked two jobs and Mom was able to stay at home, which was a great thing. When we four kids grew older, around age ten to fifteen, our father took a job with the post office, where he eventually retired. Our family always took great vacations: camping, boating, road trips to other states and national parks. It was a blast and those memories I'll always cherish.

My dad, like most, was also "the enforcer" of the household rules. You know that line, "wait till your father gets home"? Well, we heard it *a lot*. Or maybe, it was just something us kids understood without the actual words being said. As children, we knew: if we were giving Mom any grief or fighting too much, we'd be in big trouble once Dad got home. I'd say we were basically "scared" into being good kids.

Around my sixth grade, however, something in my father changed. Maybe it was the fact that my two older brothers were at those difficult teenage years. Maybe it was because memories of his own teen years resurfaced in the shadows of his psyche, and he didn't know how to disconnect from the anger, guilt, and shame of his own past. I'll never know. What I do know, however, is that's when he became more controlling of me, and physically abusive. He also was mean to my brothers, and we all suffered psychological abuse as well. After we three older kids had finally moved out, we suspect that our baby brother still living at home, was abused, too. We'll never really know for sure because sadly, we've been estranged from him for years. Whatever the reason behind our father's tumble into darkness, it happened. It's part of my past and who I am, and always will be. Except, as I grew older, I began to understand that the past is the past, and why it's important to know that.

As we grow older, the larger-than-life persona that was "Dad" fades, and we come to realize: he is/was just a man, a human being like the rest of us, not some demi-God. He had his faults, flaws, and hang-ups, and there's nothing we can do to fix that.

There comes a time in every person's life where we find ourselves at a crossroads: either continue on the path of blaming our parents for the way our lives are today, or forge out on a new path, one that offers us and our entire family lineage the formidable power of forgiveness. One that allows us to finally release the past so we can learn to love ourselves again. So, we can see and know our incredible strengths and worthiness.

This "path less traveled" is a much better road, I assure you.

I forgave my father a long time ago. His last days were spent sitting in an Alzheimer's home, memories of the abuse he inflicted—lost. It was a blessing for him, I suppose, to be free of soul-eating guilt and remorse. He spent his last days on Earth in "no time" with "no body." He lost his entire family because he refused to face himself and his demons, be account-able for his actions, and take responsibility for how he had treated his family.

I used to be sad on Father's Day. But now, I just remember the good man, the man I knew *before* whatever latched onto him (or hatched inside him) that led him to such dark, destructive places. Before he lost sight of Himself and of Love.

One morning, as the stillness of predawn awakened something inside me, I reached for my journal and wrote, "I forgive you Dad. I love the man you once were and miss *that* Dad. I hope you find peace . . . please know that I have."

Mothers have so much to teach us, and us them. As I flew up north to be with Mom for a few days, I had time to reflect on how we've communicated, loved, fought, learned, and grown. My mother has contributed to my personality, fears, dreams, and values. And, I'd like to think I've influenced hers as well.

As a child, growing up with a stay-at-home mother who could give me her full-time attention and love, I didn't really appreciate the blessing of that. Most families these days don't have that option. For many families, both parents are working, or a single, working parent has to manage it all. Not that there weren't things she could've done differently (meaning better, in my humble "non-parenting" opinion).

German-born and raised, she and my father had met during the Korean War. So, giving birth to four small children by the time she was twenty-three and raising us in a strange country where she had to learn a new language and adopt new customs must've been disorienting and lonely for her. How much, how quickly, she had to adapt kind of blows my mind. It's all I can do to manage my own life in a country I call "home," let alone raise that many small children in a strange, new culture.

I learned quite a few things from my mother: responsibility to family and friends, appreciation for nature's beauty, unconditional love, and patience.

I'd like to think that I've helped her realize a few valuable lessons, too. Like, live in the moment, Mom, and don't worry so much—about everything! Things happen in their own divine time and there are some things we have zero control over. Accept what life brings you. Trust yourself and what you want. And it's OK to toot your own horn now and then, Mom, because if you don't, who will?

Eventually, the day will come, for our roles to reverse. "Someday, I will become the caretaker, the nurturing, responsible adult that showers her with unconditional love," I journaled one morning, the coo of the turtle doves calling forth another new day. "I love you, Mom, so please be at peace knowing that."

As you go through your own healing process, family can be a great opportunity to practice setting boundaries, testing new, healthier behaviors and interactions, to see how far you have actually come in dealing with those old emotional triggers.

An unsupportive, dysfunctional family, however, should spur you to find support elsewhere. I know when I was in the depths of counseling and navigating who I wanted in my life, my circle of friends and my connection to the Universe (that I call God) was crucial. If you find yourself needing some space and time from your family to determine what YOU need and to build a stronger foundation for yourself, always listen to your heart. Tell them you love them; you just need this time to focus on your healing. Hopefully, your family will understand. And if they don't, well, maybe they're part of the problem. You may be forced to disconnect completely and create your own kind of family.

EXERCISE:
Identifying Family Feelings/Triggers

The chart below can help you pinpoint how you and your family members interact and how their energy affects you. If you determine there isn't a lot of support from your family, then do this same exercise with friends that ARE your supporters. I suggest photocopying the chart, so you have one for each family member and/or close friend. At the end of this exercise, notice who best fills your well of loving support.

- Take a few minutes to jot down here what kind of qualities you feel a healthy, loving family should have?

- Using a copy of the chart below for each family member (or friend), write his/her name across the top.

- Now, circle each person's character qualities (don't over-think it; go with your first instinct).

Notice:
- Is there anything that stands out to you, any pattern with that person?

- Who has the *most* amount of **healthy** character qualities? Who has the *least?*

- What feelings arise when you read your responses for each person?

- What person and his/her energy do you *choose* to have in your circle of influence, as part of your family?

NAME _____

Circle the character qualities you associate with each family member or friend.

ANGRY	HAPPY	ANXIOUS	RESPONSIBLE	SAD	ADVENTUROUS
Irritated	Thankful	Afraid	Wise	Hurt	Confident
Annoyed	Comfortable	Worried	Supportive	Jealous	Excited
Grumpy	Playful	Pessimistic	Honest	Depressed	Inspirational
Impatient	Trusting	Stressed	Nurturing	Pessimistic	Focused
Guilty	Content	Nervous	Loyal	Disillusioned	Proactive
Paralyzed	Optimistic	Victimized	Patient	Lonely	Creative

PART

2

The Process of
Transformation

CHAPTER
7

Who Am "I"?

"Who looks outside, dreams; who looks inside, awakes."

– Carl Jung

No matter how much you respect and value the voices of others—and that includes family and friends, mentors and teachers, therapists and spiritual advisors—none of these people can look into your heart . . . like you can.

At the end of the day, your wisest, deepest knowing of who you are *will never come from outside yourself.*

I was twenty-one before I realized that the wounds of my past were running my life and overshadowing the real ME, my "true north," a nice metaphor for one's internal compass. I had finally confessed to my husband of six months the truth of what my father had done. He insisted I seek counseling immediately.

Money was tight so my first counselor suggested group therapy. I pushed back, adamant that I was fine. *I mean, I'd already gotten this far in life, hadn't I?* I tried to persuade my husband and therapist that I could deal with what had happened to me. I wanted to forget the incest ever happened, and just get on with my life. In the end, I dragged myself to group therapy, but only to placate them both.

Naturally, I was nervous. I didn't know what to expect. This was my first ever "therapy session" and it was with a group of women who'd been sexually abused as well. I was determined to show up as "normal" (whatever that meant!). *I was nothing like those other people; I was one tough, stoic soul who'd survived a sinister past. Everyone there would see how I had rescued myself!*

I sat there and listened to stories of everyday life from nine other women. There was the young, single mother of three children on the hunt for work. She was impatient, always blaming everyone else for her stressful predicaments, and markedly insecure, lonely, afraid. She was the perfect mirror for where I was at. Another woman, sixty-five, was just beginning to remember the traumatic events of her past, and wading through a swamp of dark emotions, while grappling with deep depression. *Well, that's something else we have in common!* And, an executive who worked among a group of colleagues with strong personalities was fighting like hell to express herself and declare her own worth. Yes, I understood her battle, too.

Ahh. I started to connect the dots. All of these women were feeling anxious, afraid, and confused. We were having similar self-defeating thoughts and emotions as we struggled to make sense of life. *Maybe, just maybe there's something to this therapy thing,* I

60

thought. Maybe the abuse *had* affected "Who I Am, " my actions and behavior, and how I viewed life. *Could working through the trauma and its aftereffects help lift my depression? Is this why I hide from confrontation and avoid speaking up if I don't agree with someone? Why I feel like a "bad" person for not going along with what others say and expect of me?*

I finally realized, especially when I was young, that most of my choices hadn't come from the core of who I really am (what "I" Veronica wanted and needed). Instead, they came from the opinions of others, and what "I" thought would impress *them.*

> ***I was living a hollow kind of life that revolved around looking good, being right, and doing everything I could to win their validation.* Their love. *Nearly everything I did and said came from that wounded self.***

It shouldn't be surprising that I rarely managed to forge the kind of healthy, authentic connections I so craved. And, I sure as hell wasn't living the kind of life I'd once dreamt of. Like Mick Jagger says, "Lose your dreams and you might lose your mind." Well, through all those years of missteps, chaos, and suffering, I think deep-down inside, I *did* know—this is *not* who I want to be, and this is *not* the path I want to keep taking.

My fear of rejection drove my need for approval and love, and my desire to get those things fueled my often controlling, manipulative behavior. It was literally running (and ruining) my life. No wonder I kept on attracting the wrong men, wrong friends, wrong job. Shocker, huh? I was so utterly lost in other people's validations, sinking in shame and self-hatred that I didn't believe I was deserving of my dreams.

It wasn't until my forties, after years of seminars and absorbing books, investing in therapy and deep healing energy work that I began to develop true self-awareness and learn to listen and heed my inner voice (the one that had been there all along—before, during, and after the abuse). And then, as I kept practicing new habits (and unlearning old habits), I started to vibrate from my own true self. That's when my ship, my life . . . turned around.

Being real is hard; however, I promise: the more you practice being genuinely yourself, the easier it gets. It becomes more natural.

Somedays, it can feel like you're struggling with everything you've got just to hold onto your Self. So many outside influences, such as family, religion, society, media, and so on, want us to think, behave, and look a certain way (*their* way).

But you know what's harder? Taking those last breaths in your final days, hours, moments, knowing you have some very deep regrets. Regrets about staying and playing smaller than you knew you were. Regrets about holding onto the past, obsessing over things that didn't really matter, and withholding compassion, kindness, and love for yourself and others. Regretful that you didn't live the life . . . you really wanted.

> *Your personal powers, the ones you were born with, only reawaken once you* really feel and know who you are and are brave enough to show up as yourself. *No excuses, no apologies.*

It requires you to make conscious, responsible choices based on an honest evaluation and awareness of yourself, with zero judgment. It means keeping your heart and mind open and learning to forgive yourself and others (while holding yourself and others accountable, minus the judgment).

In the face of rejection, are you showing up as who you are, or who "they" want you to be? If there's a strong chance of betrayal, why are you holding onto a person or situation like that? Isn't it better to be accepted and loved for who you are, instead of pretending to be someone you're not?

As I said earlier, it took me years of reclaiming parts and pieces of myself on this journey back to being me—working on my wounds and confidence, my relationships and dreams— before I realized: *no one* should ever feel like they're not good enough, that they have nothing to give, or that they will never be happy. That's just a tragic story we made up to try and make sense of the horrible things that happened to us in the past. But now it's time to give it up. It's time to peel away the layers of our fear and victimhood that keep concealing who we are and only dim our Light. It's time to shine, baby, shine!

EXERCISE:
A Reality Check for Your Soul

This exercise is about practicing self-awareness. Like a reality check for your soul, it reveals where you need to course correct when you don't like where you're headed. Be kind to yourself as you work through your thoughts and feelings of the day, and the challenging moments that appear. This is about using your innate gifts to see the solution. Eventually, this kind of self-evaluation will become second nature to you. You'll catch yourself in those very moments when you're wanting to hide how you feel and just throw on a mask. Whenever a moment like that crops up (and believe me, it will), be honest, but also be gentle as you silently ask yourself:

- Is this really what I want to do?

- In my gut, does this choice feel "heavy" or "light"?

- Will others disapprove of, or judge me? Is it better to please them and lose a part of myself, or stay true to me?

- If I don't do or act the way others want me to, is it worth disappointing or hurting myself?

- Will this demonstrate to myself and others who I really am?

- Do I have other options, and are any of them who I really am?

Pay attention to your gut feelings or an intuition about people, places, and situations. Intentionally work through these questions above and you'll begin to release those negative emotions that have been draining you (literally) for far too long. Once you consciously become aware of what you're *thinking* and how you're *responding*, a portal opens that you can step through and finally free yourself from the prison of the past. Stop allowing others to define you because you're afraid they won't love you and may abandon you. Otherwise, you're only abandoning yourself! As Deepak Chopra says, "Awareness is all about restoring your freedom to choose what you want instead of what your past imposes on you."

So, ask yourself "Who am I?" Ask often. Ask from self-love. Ask from gentle honesty, self-compassion, and full accountability for your own Life. Ask and answer, not for the sake of others, but for your own.

Be the magnificent person you know you are.

CHAPTER 8

Honesty Sets You Free

*"Even if the consequence for telling the truth is rejection
from everyone I know, that's not the same death threat
that it was when I was a child. I'm a self-sufficient adult
and abandonment no longer means the end of my life."*

– Christina Enevoldsen, *The Rescued Soul*

Honesty is hard. Especially when it comes to being honest with
ourselves. Before the trauma, we were innocent children who
deserved to be nurtured, protected, loved. Except our families
failed us. They may have known or suspected and pretended
otherwise. Or, acknowledged the crime, but bizarrely minimized
it. They may have threatened us if we ever told anyone or denied it
even happened. For some of us, there may have been relatives,
friends, or neighbors who would've jumped in to protect us, if only
they'd known the truth.

"People don't need to be forced to grow," Ellen Bass writes in
The Courage to Heal: A Guide for Women Survivors of Child

Sexual Abuse. "All we need is favorable circumstances: respect, love, **honesty**, and the space to explore."

At this point, I'd like to share with you my own story about how I *thought* I was being honest about the shadows of my past that lingered inside me and ran my life. By age twenty-six, I'd gone to several counselors, but still wasn't feeling any better about my life or the direction I was headed. Therapy wasn't working. I found myself constantly haunted by the abuse, acting out in promiscuous ways in a blind and desperate attempt to find what might be "real love." I dragged myself through the swamps of depression, those suicidal thoughts lurking nearby. I refused to try medication. *They (the therapists) aren't fixing my feelings*, I thought angrily. *I'm still not good enough. I'm still lost!* It got so bad that I tumbled into a deep pit of despair, crying myself to sleep every night and thinking, *Oh my God, I'll never climb out of this hellhole, will I?* Yet, I was determined to overcome the trauma without numbing out on drugs or booze.

I was fed up and desperate for a clue. *Something's not right . . . something's missing.* Of course, sometimes, you just get a bad therapist. But four in a row? Even in my twenties, I knew better. So, one chilly evening, I sat in my one-bedroom apartment, curled up in a corner of my dilapidated second-hand sofa, a blanket tucked around me, and listened to my first two-hour taped session with Howard, my latest therapist.

I had heard about Howard through the Viscott Center, a clinic touting a new, revolutionary type of therapy. Psychiatrist David Viscott was one of the early stars of shrink radio and his style of counseling in the 1980s was known as the "Viscott method." Per the Viscott format, the therapist helped the patient reason his or her way through the trauma. The sessions were taped with permission, so that the patient could reabsorb it for themselves later and uncover their own revelations. The method revolved around three basic elements: speed, simplicity, and a dogged pursuit of the truth. Viscott's approach was all about revealing the truth of what had happened, head-on. No months or years of talk therapy, or thousands of dollars, trying to mine your way through your own damn mind.

> **As David Viscott once said, "There is no secret to surviving happily. The best way to cope is to live through pain and experience it."**

Before I'd reached the end of that first taped session with Howard, it hit me like a brick to the head: almost every answer I'd given him was about me trying to "look" right, trying to prove I was a strong person despite the horrific trauma, and doing just "fine." When I heard myself talking, over and over on those tapes, it was like listening to a defense attorney making a case for how well-adjusted and normal the defendant (me) really was—even after growing up in a crazy, dysfunctional home where my own father had molested and raped me, repeatedly.

Damaged? *Not me.*

Still hurting? *No, I'm way past that.*

Terrified of the future? *Not really, I pretty much have my shit together.*

It was obvious: I wanted to show him that I was smarter and far more resilient than most other survivors. *Honestly, what the hell was I even doing in therapy?*

Like a computer program that's finished downloading, it finally clicked in my brain, my aha moment: *Oh my God, I wasn't being honest at all about how I really felt.* I was only playing a role, the superwoman role, and wearing a pretty clever mask to disguise the shame, guilt, anger, and confusion. Even though I had revealed the abuse, something was still rotting inside me—and I didn't want to reveal *that shit* to anyone, not even a professional. This lightning bolt of awareness woke me up: I was *never* going to get a handle on my negative emotions and *never* get a chance to heal—if I couldn't be honest about *all* of it. Certainly, no counselor holds the key to some secret portal that you could simply walk through and discover a fulfilling, happy life. There was no magic playbook to fix this kind of wound—not unless I decided to reveal *all of my pain.*

Back then, appearing "strong" to the rest of the world was more important to me than sharing and healing my deepest pain. Mostly because asking for help only reinforced my false beliefs that, "I'm not good enough," "I'm flawed," and "I'm weak." I was trying to control how others saw me, so I could contain the depths of that pain. Here I was, pretending to be a strong, young woman who'd survived horrific abuse as a child, with barely a scar or internal damage.

But it was a lie.

I decided to hit the reset button with my therapist and promised to be completely honest with myself and him. Otherwise, there was no way in hell he could help me . . . help myself. I needed to shine a light on those dark fears and negative beliefs that were driving (and ruining) my life. I needed to become aware of what was really happening under the hood of my psyche.

Believe me, if you're not being honest about what you're feeling and experiencing in life, you're going to keep making decisions based on irrational fears and limiting beliefs that are holding you back.

These self-defeating thoughts are psychological roadblocks that stop you from living your own life—**they are <u>not</u> reality!**

Honesty is the golden key that unlocks the portal to your true powers and the choices you make. Honesty is the fuse that ignites your awareness of your power—and the potential of your life!

So, I ask, "Are you really honoring YOURSELF by making excuses for others? Do you keep showing up as some super hero(ine) that doesn't need anyone's help? Or, are you afraid to even ask for it? Are you really looking at the situation with a clear head and heart? Are you ready (and willing) to see the truth of how amazing you are?

Because let's face it. If you're not being honest about what you're feeling regarding a person, place, or situation, and refuse to change whatever you need to change, then my fellow survivor, you're likely hanging onto your excuses because they are what have defined you so far—and it's effin' scary to let go of *that*.

I don't mean to make it sound so easy. But if you're *not* being honest about *your* feelings and truths, you won't be the one doing the choosing. Instead, your choices will tend to come from a people-pleasing, hollow place. Don't be so busy denying and numbing the past that you're not being honest about how it still impacts you today. Only you hold the Power to create your own kind of Life, the way that you like it. *It's time to lift the lantern.*

A long time ago, we made up a story that
we were abused because something must have
been wrong with us. You know that tape in your
head, the one that's constantly believing, "If only
I'd been . . . (fill in the blank)." Well, it's not the truth.

Whenever you listen to those critical, misguided voices, you're *believing a lie.* You're allowing these negative voices from the past to mess up your life, today. It's time to stop holding onto lies of unworthy, less-than, unlovable. It's time to be honest with yourself, and to reveal these lies for what they are: total B.S.! It's time to set yourself free.

EXERCISE:
Dropping the Mask

Journaling is a great way to reveal what's true for you, what's behind your own mask. As you jot down whatever thoughts and feelings arise the most, the ones that trigger you, you'll become more aware of their power over you—and then you can see them for what they are: thoughts and beliefs we created while trying to make sense of traumatic events. These thoughts and beliefs are not who you are, so it's vital to bring them to the surface and examine them honestly and with self-compassion. Review the questions below and write out whatever thoughts and feelings appear, as well as your reactions to those feelings.

- Do you wear the mask of denial, insisting that *I'm OK, I can handle "it,"* whatever it is, when in fact, you could really use some outside support or a wise ear to just listen?

- Do you feel like you'd be a bother if you reached out for support or to express yourself?

  - What is the thought behind that feeling? (e.g., I'm not worth it, I'm weak, etc.)

  - Whenever you react from that feeling, are you trying to be right, validate your worth, be liked, or loved?

  - Do you harshly judge yourself for having these feelings in the first place?

  - Are you escaping, numbing out, and using distractions or addictions (e.g., alcohol, drugs, shopping, sex, TV, work, etc.) to avoid these feelings?

CHAPTER
9

Forgiveness Is for You

*"Your forgiving someone doesn't erase the consequences
. . . you are doing this 'forgiving' for you, so that you can
get off your grudge and get your life on the road."*
– Dr. Ron Smothermon, *Winning Through Enlightenment*

Forgiveness is a powerful, yet often misunderstood practice—one
that can be tricky to wrap our heads and hearts around. After all,
if the act of forgiveness can't undo what's already been done, or
make the perpetrator accountable and bring us justice, then why
is it so necessary to heal the worst wounds imaginable?

Here's why: Because holding onto that pain and anger not only
drains you of energy and vitality, it also keeps you *stuck*.

**By refusing to practice forgiveness, you actually
stand in the way of your own well-being.
Grudges are toxic and have never healed anyone.**

Those who consider themselves spiritual, and people of different faiths, understand the power of forgiveness to heal and create lasting change on a deep, metaphysical level.

But it turns out, there's a scientific reason, too. Researchers have found that forgiveness improves our mental and physical health. Those who learn to forgive actually experience less stress, reduced anxiety and depression, increased energy, and even a stronger immune system.[7] Because grudges never end up hurting the person who hurt us. They only hurt us. Year after year, holding onto a grudge only bleeds out your same wound.

As survivors of abuse, trauma, and other painful childhood experiences, over time, we naturally invented stories about our own identity . . . "I must be weak . . . stupid . . . ugly," and so on. We were only trying to make sense of *why* we were unloved, violated, and abandoned by our family or those we trusted, in the first place. Some of us may hold onto these negative self-beliefs as a way to manipulate others through self-pity and seeming like a helpless person. Or, we may even redirect any attention from our own bad behaviors and choices onto others. Forever playing the blame game, stuck in a constant state of victimhood, while avoiding responsibility for our own choices as adults.

Sure, I had managed to survive a traumatic
childhood and rescue myself. Except, I was
still acting out in some stupid, self-destructive
ways and repeating the same dysfunctional patterns.

7. Kirsten Weir, "Forgiveness can improve mental and physical health: research show how to get there," *American Psychological Association* (January 2017) Vol. 48, No. 1

I kept choosing men who were unavailable, selfish, or totally not into me so I could validate how unlovable I was. I cared more about everyone else because I believed that they were more important than me. I continued to cling to self-pity and justifiable rage. *My father ruined my life, dammit! Look how messed up I am! I fucking hate him!* And, the very thought of forgiving him (and myself) had me spinning on a wheel of constant chaos, bringing me even more pain, confusion, and heartache.

I remember the day when my therapist Howard gently suggested, "Veronica, it may be time to look at how you feel about forgiving your father."

I was thirty-five and well into my journey of understanding just how much my childhood trauma had been the one directing my thoughts and beliefs about myself and others, and the possibilities of my own life. When he first suggested this, however, my stomach twisted. *How could I forgive him if I was still afraid of him?* Just the year before, I had seen him in a car on the freeway and practically drove off the road, so shaken that he might see me, hunt me down and try to hurt me.

> ***Here's the truth. I felt sick at the thought
> of forgiving him—*** **but I knew I was ready to.
> *I knew that holding onto that pain and
> continuing to live as a victim was hurting me.***

So, I asked myself, "Who do you want to be *now*, Veronica?" *Why* would I continue to let "him" rule my choices and beliefs about who I am and how I live my life? I was in control now, not him. I had compassion for myself. This was a huge step in my own healing; it gave me permission to take charge of my life, to own my actions, thoughts, and beliefs that for far too long had been triggered by these old feelings and abusive patterns.

You mean I have the power? I can decide right now to be loving, decisive, and happy regardless of the past? Forgiving him meant that I no longer needed to cling to those wounds—that I could finally decide for myself who I really was.

Soon after, I arranged to meet my father at Conrad's, a classic diner in Pasadena. It was right down the street from where I lived. He didn't know that, however, so I felt safe meeting him there. When I first saw him, all the emotions of the past—distrust, anger, pain, disappointment, and unworthiness flooded forth and nearly knocked me off my feet. He was sitting in a corner booth, frail and much older than I remembered in the seven years since I had last seen him. We exchanged the superficial "how are yous" and mundane weather comments to avoid any emotional outbursts. When we were ready to leave, he said, "I want to give you something." We walked out to his car and he went to open the trunk. My mind started racing with visions of him shoving me in, driving to some mountain top, and throwing me over a cliff.

Instead when he opened the trunk, I saw a box.

"I want you to have these."

Inside were three dozen VHS tapes, all home movies of my family's life, from my oldest to my youngest brother, and all the years in-between. My family's entire story as told by my father in pictures. Of course, the irony here is what those pictures didn't say.

Then, he glanced down at his feet, and croaked out, "I'm so sorry."

He started to cry uncontrollably, and, then in my caretaker fashion, I said, "It's all right Dad. I'm OK." My knee-jerk response was an ingrained attempt to take care of *his* feelings (not mine), and I instantly knew I'd have to let him take full responsibility, not let him off the hook. So, I corrected my words right away, "I'm OK, *despite what happened.*"

In the end, I got what I wanted and needed for decades: his admission and sorrow for the horrific pain and abuse he had caused.

Today, I can say that I've forgiven my dad whose last days were lived out in an Alzheimer's home, alone in his own darkness, remembering nothing. And, I've forgiven my mother, as well. I have empathy for her: she's in her own self-imposed prison, refusing to forgive herself for failing to protect me, and sadly remains unhappy, deeply depressed, and haunted by unfulfilled dreams. She's tortured the most. I think about how much happier she could be if she'd acknowledge what happened, take responsibility for her part, and then choose to forgive herself completely, and appreciate all the good that she has done in the world. She'd then be living for today, instead of mired in the past.

Of course, forgiving ourselves is the hardest of all, but also the most important. There are those who feel forgiving the perpetrator isn't essential for their healing, and I agree. However, *forgiving yourself is essential.* I had to forgive myself for all the mistakes I'd made as a young woman. For not speaking up and telling a relative, neighbor, teacher, or any adult who could have stepped in and stopped my father's assaults. For feeling that I'd somehow brought this on myself or deserved it. And, finally, I had to forgive myself for being helpless to protect that little, innocent girl, the one who believed she could do anything. I had to tell her: *it's OK now; you're with me and I will always protect you.* The child who felt invincible and safe, happily pedaling her bike, that red cape flapping in the breeze.

> *Learning to forgive yourself is the only way to move on with your life and release the painful past. Otherwise, we unconsciously continue to act from our hurt and wounded self, allowing that damn past to dictate our present and future.*

"Without our deserving it, we can experience thunderous injustices," notes Bob Enright, a psychologist at the University of Wisconsin, Madison, and an early pioneer on the study of forgiveness. "The injury was unfair; the person who created it was unfair. But now we have a place for healing."[8]

Once you choose to forgive, you take back your power. You free yourself from the shackles of the past and start to create the life you've always wanted. It's never too late to forgive, to make amends with yourself and others, and to find your way back.

MEDITATION: THE STREAM OF RELEASING

I wrote this to help you release any negative thoughts and replace them with only positive thoughts. Visualization is a powerful tool for personal transformation. I urge you to record this first, so you can play it back, listen and fully experience this deeply healing meditation. This is not a one-time practice. Try and do "The Stream of Releasing" once a week, if you can.

Close your eyes and get comfortable. Draw attention to your breathing, noticing the rising and falling of your abdomen or chest, the air flowing in and out through your nose or mouth.

---

8. Ibid.

Think the words, "Breathing in . . . breathing out." Don't worry if you get distracted by thoughts or feelings; just remain focused on your breathing. If your attention has wandered, simply come back to your breath. Take several deep breaths, inhaling and exhaling fully.

Now, imagine you're walking along a trail that leads you into a beautiful emerald-green forest. You see leaves swaying in the breeze, feel the soft wind on your face just as the sun is breaking through the trees.

With your next breath, you notice a clearing. As you draw closer to the clearing you see a slow-moving stream. It gurgles gently. The water is so clear you can see the sandy bottom. It's only a foot deep and you feel the urge to step into the stream. As your feet enter the stream, you stand there, glancing left, then right, taking in a clear upstream/downstream view. The water tugs at you gently, and you feel content as the stream flows around your legs. It's mildly cool, refreshing. You feel relaxed and peaceful and turn your head to the right to watch the water make its way downstream through the forest.

You take another deep breath, and with that breath, notice any thoughts that arise. If the thoughts are negative or make you anxious, worried, or scared, simply observe them. Then look left, upstream, to the horizon of the stream. You see a piece of paper floating, and instantly know this paper has your negative thought(s) written on it as it carries all the feelings you were having. As it floats toward you, notice how it looks: How big is it, what shape is it, is it white or some other color? Is the paper flat or crumpled? As your eyes follow the paper coming toward you, you can feel the impact of the thought(s), whatever that emotion is for you. As it reaches you, you take another deep breath and say, "Thank you for the delivery of that thought. I release any worry and pain, and only accept love and compassion. I am now at peace."

You watch as the piece of paper floats past you, carrying all your worry, fear, and pain with it. You only feel the water on your legs now. Take another deep breath. See what other thought arises for you and watch as another piece of paper floats toward you. You repeat these same words as it reaches and drifts past you: "Thank you for the delivery of that thought. I release any worry and pain, and only accept love and compassion. I am now at peace."

After a while you will feel and observe that no more negative thoughts are coming downstream; only positive, loving thoughts. Here comes one now, and you think, "I am strong." And then another, "I am determined," and another, "I am Love," and on and on. You smile softly when you see that all these positive thought-papers have floated up onto the shore right in front of you.

You slowly move out of the stream toward the pile of positive thought-papers waiting for you on the riverbank. You gather them up, thanking the stream for its infinite wisdom and for helping you release the negative thoughts and replacing them with positive thoughts.

It's time to head back. You take the same trail out of the forest, your positive, loving notes in hand.

CHAPTER 10

Surrender Thou Judgments

"A day spent judging another is a painful day.
A day spent judging yourself is a painful day."

– Buddha

Here's the tricky thing about the mind: It's going to judge. We judge others and we judge ourselves all the time. Except, here's the kicker: our judgments aren't based on facts and reality; they aren't the same as the Truth.

We judge in all sizes and ways. A close friend forgets our birthday, so we decide that she's selfish. A driver cuts us off in traffic and we assume he did it intentionally. A business associate forgets to return our call, and we think, *I must not be that important.* (This last one has to do with us—judging us.)

Judgment is a human emotion, one that starts as a thought and spirals out from there. Ever try and stop a thought . . . once you've thought it? Impossible. But the problem with judgment is that it keeps us isolated, separate from others and ourselves. It slams doors far too quickly on people, places, and things we know very little about; we just *assume* we do. We often misread what's going on with another person. We assume that we know what other cultures, political parties, and religions are really like. Or, we criticize other people's occupations, interests, and lifestyles—without ever getting to know them at all.

> *Over the years, judging becomes a destructive*
> *habit, one we unconsciously fall into. It's*
> *our mind's way of trying to find some quick*
> *resolution to an uncomfortable feeling, or an*
> *attempt to cover up its own insecurities and fears.*

We also judge others to feel better about ourselves. *I would never do that! . . . At least, I'm not that bad! . . . They must be crazy,* and so on. And, at the time, we don't even know that we're doing it. Except later, something doesn't feel quite right in our gut, once we've judged. You know the feeling.

Let me be clear: I'm not talking about evaluating whether a person, place, or thing is good for you, or not. That's actually using your head, in a smart, healthy way. As an adult, you need to assess the situation, then choose how to act accordingly.

But judging? It's a different kind of beast. A pain-in-the-ass beast that annoys and hurts others and invents stories based on false assumptions and opinions.

> *Ultimately, the judgment habit inhibits our*
> *ability to trust others and make deeper*
> *connections. It stunts our mental, emotional,*
> *and spiritual growth, and keeps us playing small.*

More often than not, what's going on with another person has nothing to do with us—it's about their pain, their struggle. Like Will Smith says, "Never underestimate the pain of a person because in all honesty, everyone is struggling. Some people are better at hiding it than others."

In his groundbreaking book, *The Seven Habits of Highly Effective People*, the late Dr. Stephen R. Covey shared a personal story to illustrate how we often misjudge what's going on with others and their situation. One Sunday morning, Covey was riding a New York City subway and everyone in the train was quiet and peaceful, some reading the newspaper, and others just resting. That is, until a man and his three children hopped aboard. The kids started arguing and running wild around the train, while their father, seated next to Covey, mutely stared at the floor. As the minutes ticked by, the children became more obnoxious, grabbing newspapers and openly disturbing the other passengers.

Finally, Covey had had enough. He turned to the guy and asked him to speak with his children and make them behave. The father gazed up at Covey in confusion as if he was from another planet. Then, he softly replied that Covey was right; he should do something. They'd just left the hospital where their mother had died just an hour ago. The father confessed he was utterly lost, and realized that his kids were, too. At that moment, Covey got it: he had completely misjudged this man as a neglectful parent with unruly kids. How wrong he had been. Suddenly, Covey could feel the man's deepest pain, and his irritation transformed into compassion and empathy.

I think if "judgment" had a polar opposite, it would be "empathy." Empathy is the capacity to step inside the shoes of others and imagine what it feels like—to be *them*. But judgment? It loves to make those righteous snap verdicts as if we know the truth of everyone and everything. Which we don't.

As a certified Leadership and Life Coach, I often work with women who, despite their amazing career and business successes, still struggle to find their voice, to speak and live their truth, and respond in a healthy way to crisis or change. Instead, they often get triggered by deep-seated, destructive self-talk, such as "I'm not good enough," "not smart enough," "too old," and *blah blah blah* prattles on that stupid judge inside our heads. But this judgmental voice does nothing to improve and transform our situation or dilemma; in fact, it will only sidetrack or even block the forward momentum we need to make—especially whenever a big life whammy comes along that shakes us up (e.g., divorce, retirement, empty nest syndrome, or death of a partner or someone close). I've found that underneath our internal struggles lurks an ingrained, *unconscious* habit of being overly self-critical and self-judgmental. These women are harder on themselves than anyone else, doing constant battle with themselves. I understand (all too well) that their tendency to self-judge (not self-assess) is rooted in the traumas of the past, which had given in long ago to self-defeating, false beliefs of shame, guilt, and unworthiness.

Whenever you catch yourself judging, start to replace it with the healing habit of nonjudgment. Nonjudgment allows you to observe and assess what's happening without the murky fog of negativity and misperceptions that got created a long, long time ago. Nonjudgment is a critical step toward creating a newfound awareness of how powerful our thoughts really are. We don't have to let that old, inner judge run our lives *anymore*.

I promise, once you start to shift your judgmental thoughts to nonjudgmental, empathic thoughts, something incredible happens:

You open a portal that connects your mind and body to your inner being, your Higher Self, your soul! (Please, don't get hung up on semantics here; feel free to use any word that resonates for *you*). Your inner being or soul already knows that you are *not* alone in this world. That you *are* worthy of feeling safe, loved, and joyful. (And, by the way, you don't need to earn it—that's just another made-up story from the dysfunctional past!). When you start to feel the love and truth that is *really you*—who you were born as— you'll discover there's no more need to act out with drama, anger, blame, and withdrawal. There's no more need to prove to yourself, and others, that you're worthy of love. Because one day, you'll just *know* it.

At first, this other voice inside you is harder to hear, especially the longer you've been letting the voices of doubt, shame, and unworthiness dominate the conversations in your head. That wiser voice of yours, however, knows the real you: your path, your worth, your unique beauty.

> *Whenever we look at the world through the clearer lens of nonjudgment and empathy, we begin to see all **our potential and possibilities. There are no limits.***

EXERCISE:
Don't Judge, Be Curious

Imagine what would happen if you opened your heart to your own spirit, and stopped the destructive habit of judging? As Mother Teresa so simply, yet profoundly put it, "If you judge people, you have no time to love them." That includes yourself.

Being nonjudgmental takes practice. This exercise is power- fully eye- and heart-opening. When I first tried this, I had just had my own lesson about misjudging others after interviewing a smart candidate for a major healthcare medical group. She had a great resume, and entered my office dressed beautifully in a fitted blue suit with a take-charge demeanor. About ten minutes in, however, I was starting to sense hostility from her. Her answers were good but too short and guarded. As the minutes ticked by, her tone grew markedly terse. I finally put down the resume and was quite direct with her.

"I'm sorry," I looked her in the eye. "Your resume and experience are exactly what we're looking for." I paused. "But I have to tell you; all I am getting right now is an attitude of anger."

Her face relaxed and her shoulders instantly softened as the tension escaped her body like a deflated balloon. "I'm so sorry," she shook her head, her voice softer. "It's been so long since I've been on an interview. I'm just so nervous and scared."

Our brief, honest exchange had turned everything around and I hired her on the spot.

I realized that I had misjudged her and what was really going on with her. That moment was so awakening for me that I decided from that point forward to also observe myself whenever I started to judge someone else. It takes conscious practice. But learning to become aware of how we not only judge others, but also ourselves, is well worth it, I promise you.

SO, READY TO FLEX YOUR NONJUDGMENT MUSCLES?

Pick a crowded place, where a lot of people walk by (e.g., a mall or park, an airport or street café). Sit where you can see everyone, and everyone can see you. Now silently choose to open your heart to everyone that passes by. With each person, say silently to yourself (so others won't start staring and judging you—ha), "I see you, and I love you just the way you are." Breathe deeply and allow yourself to feel that person's heart, presence, and energy. Then, move on to someone else.

Yes, you'll still have judgmental thoughts popping up. Don't worry. Just acknowledge the thoughts, and then let them go, while saying to yourself, "I see you, and I love you just the way you are." You may be curious about why some people act or dress a certain way. "I wonder why she's crying?" Don't judge it, just be softly curious. "Why does he look mad?" Don't judge it; just be softly curious. Keep replacing and releasing any judgmental thoughts with the same phrase, "I see you, and I love you just the way you are."

I can't tell you how present and powerful you'll feel once you do this. The connection to others is incredible! But you won't really know until you discover it for yourself. I urge you to journal about your experience and the wave of emotions that hit you, both during and after this exercise.

CHAPTER
11

Learn to Trust Again

*"Logic becomes a loud voice when the wall of
our past abuse begins to crack with awareness.
But that's our adult speaking. The child
within, who had the experience, talks to
us through flashes of insights. Trust your
perceptions. They are a powerful guide in healing."*

– Jeanne McElvaney, *Childhood Abuse*

Trust, a necessary but tenuous bond, is at the center of all
relationships.

As children, we developed our sense of trust and safety
from family and other adults. We quickly discovered who we
could trust and who we couldn't. So, it's no surprise that as
child sexual abuse survivors, we've had a tougher time trusting
others and ourselves than the non-abused. What happened to
us was the ultimate betrayal.

Throughout childhood and adolescence,
we sadly adopted these negative beliefs
about ourselves, taking the blame and
believing it must be our fault. It was the only
way we could cope and make sense of the victimization.

The problem, however, is that as adult survivors, we can continue to carry these scars from our past into our present. What I call the Hurt-Wounded Self stands guard, in fear that others will continue to hurt us. We also tend to mistrust our own instincts and judgment.

For me, I realized that I had to start loving myself *first*, before I could learn to trust myself. In my twenties, I remember feeling that I just wasn't important enough, or valued enough as a person, to speak up when I needed to, or to have an opinion. I was so afraid of being judged and unloved by others. Truth is, I hadn't yet learned to love and trust myself again, which is why I couldn't fully express who I was, what I wanted and needed. Many times, I'd put the needs and wants of others far above my own. Unknowingly, I had abandoned myself. Of course, repressing my voice and holding back only made me feel worse, not to mention, it was pretty exhausting to not be myself.

Once you start to honor, respect, and
unconditionally *love who you are, your*
behavior and actions can't help but change
accordingly, and so will everything else
in your life. Because at this point, you're
learning to make choices and take
action from a strong sense of self-trust.

You'll realize that it's healthy to set personal boundaries for your own sake. You'll worry less and release your grip on the need to control everything and everyone. You'll learn to listen to your own guidance system, which helps you see people, places, and situations more clearly (without the distorted lens of childhood trauma), and you'll know who and what you can trust. You'll begin to trust your feelings without being a victim to them or making someone else a victim by overreacting in the moment.

As the great poet and novelist Goethe once said, "Just trust yourself, then you will know how to live." Learn to trust yourself again, and in turn, you'll change how you respond to any mistrustful thought you have—because you'll "know" whether that thought is coming from past trauma or current reality.

When you learn to Trust again, you shine your Light.

TIPS:

Learning to trust yourself and others takes practice, a shift in your mindset, and a deeper self-awareness. Here are some ways you can restore trust in yourself and others.

- Heed your own inner voice and listen carefully
- Disregard your inner voice if it's abusing you, criticizing you, and making you feel less-than
- Communicate your true feelings to those closest to you
- Journal how you feel about trust issues
- Take the risk to trust yourself and others; if it doesn't work out, then see it as a learning experience not to be repeated with that person or place

- Use affirmations like these to combat self-defeating, doubtful thoughts:

  o I trust my intuition

  o I trust facts and know how to evaluate important information

  o I know the difference between my past trauma and my current reality

  o I'm in charge of my thoughts, not the other way around

  o I trust not only in myself, but something bigger than myself

  o I know there are trustworthy people who love me

  o I am a trustworthy person

CHAPTER
12

Take Responsibility & Change Your Life

*"The final forming of a person's
character lies in their own hands."*

– Anne Frank

Reclaiming your power means you must start taking responsibility for your own life.

**I really want you to hear this: You're no
longer a victim. You're a grownup now,
albeit one who survived some pretty serious crap.**

It can be difficult at first to start accepting responsibility for our own thoughts, feelings, choices, and actions. I'm certainly not talking about taking responsibility for what happened to us in the past. When preyed upon as a child, we had zero choice but to endure the surrealistic hell in which we were trapped. During our transformative years, however, we bought into this illusion that we'd always be a victim. Then, we unwittingly carried this victim-hood consciousness into our adulthood.

You know that old saying, "When you point a finger at someone else, there are three fingers pointing back at you." Well, let's look at those fingers. The one pointing the blame at someone else says, "This is your fault, not mine." What if we looked at the other three and asked ourselves these three questions: *What* happened here? *Why* did it happen? *How* do I want to handle this? This is where our power lies—in reflecting on what went wrong and how we played a part in it. Then deciding what we can do about it.

Some say this expression originated in the Navajo culture that frowns upon pointing the forefinger at anyone. Even in a Navajo court of law, the judge will reprimand and remind you: there are always three pointing back at ya, sister! (OK, maybe a Navajo judge wouldn't say it quite like that, but you get the idea). Let's take those three fingers pointing back, and examine them more closely: 1) we're not taking any responsibility or holding ourselves accountable for our part in the upset or unhappiness we feel; 2) we're letting those old insecurities (the Hurt-Wounded Self) get the best of us and trying to cover them up; and 3) we've forgotten who we really are and what we stand for; otherwise, we wouldn't be so caught up deflecting, acting helpless, and blaming others.

Sure, we're human, so we're going to get caught up in the heat of the moment and make mistakes. That's part of life. But here's the key: when you do screw up, be accountable for your part. I'm not saying own all of it (unless you know you should). But look at your part—and then own it. How many times have you been upset, disappointed, or hurt, and tell yourself and others that it was someone's fault?

As author, philosopher, and musician Criss Jami puts it, "Like crying wolf, if you keep looking for sympathy as a justification for your actions, you will someday be left standing alone when you really need help."

Sometimes taking responsibility stops us cold because we may feel it's too daunting to admit when we did something wrong or are too nervous to take a stand for ourselves. Or, maybe we're afraid that others will judge us for making a choice they won't like (and dang it, we want others to like us so much!). We often fear the pain of rejection or having to face something painful about ourselves (or at least, how we've perceived ourselves, e.g., worthless, stupid, lazy, etc.).

In the moment, it seems far less painful to blame someone else for where we're at in life. But the ironic part is, the sooner we start taking full responsibility for who we are being, moment to moment, and own our choices, the sooner we reclaim our own power, clarity, and strength.

We give away our power whenever we make excuses, blame others all the time, and don't take responsibility as an adult. It's time to stop being a slave to your limiting thoughts and get off the Hurt-Wounded track, which impacts every aspect of your life: your relationships and well-being, your goals and dreams, and ultimately, your precious life-force energy.

Starting today, give yourself permission to make responsible choices for YOU, not from the grip of the past.

Whenever you take full responsibility for your choices you will:

- Feel empowered and confident in who you are

- Stop seeking outside validation just to feel good about yourself and your choices

- Build strength from within, and *feel the power of choice*

- Know exactly who you are and what you have to offer, proudly, no matter what other people may say or do

- Give yourself permission to live the life you want

- Feel more grounded and trusting about life

- Feel deserving of the fabulous life you're building and grateful for what you already have

EXCERCISE:
Stepping Up & Owning It

Here are some questions to help reveal any hidden beliefs about what responsibility means to you. Reflect on these questions and visualize yourself taking responsibility for your choices and actions. This will open the portal to you making more conscious choices—not from victimhood consciousness—but from the source of your own true Power. You'll discover an exhilarating freedom you never expected. Because taking responsibility is *life-changing*.

- What choices do you feel weren't your own, but forced upon you?

- Looking back, can you think of other choices available to you at the time?

- What new choices could you make?

- Who do you want to be today, from this point forward?

- Are you showing up for yourself by taking full responsibility for your actions and choices? If not, what area(s) do you need to step up to and fully own?

CHAPTER 13

Make Your Choices Your Own

"Life is about choices. Some we regret,
some we're proud of. Some will haunt us forever.
The message: we are what we choose to be."

– Graham Brown

The abuser takes away a child's power because the child has no choice but to suffer and endure the assault. As adult survivors, in theory, we should have pulled ourselves out of the shadow of oppression a long time ago. Except, what usually happens is that we unwittingly continue to live in the shadows of our past, holding onto a deeply flawed premise that we will always be victims, helpless to the whims of fate with very little personal choice about how we respond to stress and adversity, whom we love and spend our precious time with, and basically, who we want to be and what we really want from life.

"The world can look like a series of locked doors to adult survivors of child sexual abuse," writes Kris Bein in a paper published by the Resource Sharing Project, a nationwide move ment of sexual violence-related services and resources.[9]

Take it from me: you can waste decades
of your life believing and acting as if
you are still that powerless child-victim
and have no choice(s), from the smallest
to the biggest decisions of your life.
But this just ain't true. The irony is, if
you keep on allowing fears and wounds
of the past to control you, you're still
making a choice—a choice to live a
life that falls way short of what it could be!

YOUR "HURT-WOUNDED SELF" NO LONGER GETS TO CHOOSE

Most of our fears originated in our childhood back story, the one that keeps on tapping out these countless critical, nonconstructive messages inside our skulls, such as "I'm not lovable" . . . "I'm a bad person" . . . "I'm weak," and so on.

Yes, once upon a time, we were victims. But you know what? We're not any more.

So, why does what I call the **Hurt-Wounded Self** get to keep on running your show? Why allow this Hurt-Wounded Self even one more minute to devalue and diminish the magnificent person

---

9. Kris Bein, "Action Engagement, Remembering: Services for Adult Survivors of Child Sexual Abuse," ReShape newsletter, National Sexual Assault Coalition Resource Sharing Project, 2011.

you are? I mean, hey, it's not even qualified! The Hurt-Wounded Self's opinions and beliefs about "you" were shaped early on by the abuse and the abuser's lies—*never the truth.*

What if your past no longer gets to define your conscious mind's choices? What if today is the day you put your foot down to the Universe (and yourself!) and make the choice to move that Hurt-Wounded Self from the driver's seat to the backseat of your life? As William Ernest Henley so profoundly wrote in his poem *Invictus* (the one that Nelson Mandela drew hope from all those years in prison), "Out of the night that covers me, black as the pit from pole to pole, I thank whatever gods may be for my unconquerable soul . . . . It matters not how strait the gate, how charged with punishments the scroll; I am the master of my fate, I am the captain of my soul."

Until we practice pausing to reflect and feel where our thoughts and feelings really come from, our choices will tend to be knee-jerk responses that have nothing to do with our adult self. Make your choices and own them. Once you start doing that, your life can't help but transform for the better. You can't help but move toward what you really want and who you really are.

Traumas of the past taught us to abandon our feelings, judge ourselves, numb out, and hold others responsible for our life today. It was our way of controlling the pain. But we abandon ourselves whenever we do this and it ultimately makes us feel like crap, isolated, and unloved. We ache for others' approval, validation, and unconditional love.

> *Hidden deep in the corners of our subconscious mind, trauma-induced fear can influence our thoughts and beliefs, and cause us to us react on autopilot, like we have "no choice."*

Positive change happens once we begin to unearth the real reasons that we're fearful about money and career, health and relationships, and feel stuck in life. It may not be pretty (actually, I can pretty much guarantee it), but until we face our true feelings about a situation and fully examine our choices and options from the outside-in, we'll never feel free.

My own road to change has been a bumpy ride of emotions: from fear and excitement, to pain and doubt, and back again to fear and excitement. As a child, I dreamt of being a creative person, an artist, singer, and actress. When I finally started performing again in my teen years it was more from a needy place of craving validation and love—*not* from a deeper place of expressing who I really was and making a positive contribution to others. Whenever there was criticism or a lack of recognition around my performance, the pain I felt was almost unbearable, and reinforced my dark feelings of worthlessness and isolation. This reaction to not feeling loved or accepted stemmed from the shame and pain of the past, and the self-deprecating, negative talk in my head that "I was bad" or "I deserved this bad thing that happened," etc. As the years ticked by, it was exhausting to keep on proving my value as a human being. I made the decision in my twenties to work with a therapist, plus a group of survivors, and read as many self-improvement, inspirational books as I could get my hands on. Little by little, I was discovering what was behind these unconscious choices. It was like emotional and spiritual alchemy, changing cheap metal into pure gold. Once I began to see *why* I did what I did whenever interacting with others and *how* I chose to deal with the situation, I realized I could choose differently. Hey, what a concept!

The introspection and courage to look honestly at myself, thoughts, and action was, at times, quite painful. And yet, in the end, liberating.

Sometimes I would uncover a part of me I wasn't proud of, such as gossiping just to feel a sense of belonging and be part of the crowd. I realized that I had to start taking responsibility for how I treated others and stop blaming or playing the victim because, dammit, continuing to act like a victim only kept me stuck. I made a choice, a promise to myself, that I wasn't going to do anything I didn't I want to, just to be liked, accepted, or avoid being judged. It was high time to follow my own heart and stay confident in my own choices. When I started to attract attention as a singer, I was doubly tested on this promise to own my choices—for me—not for others.

Whenever I received a compliment or felt like I was owning my talents, I'd hear my mother's old warnings of "Don't toot your own horn" and "Be humble, no one needs to know how good you are." They never go away totally; I've just learned through practice to ignore them. Always remember: You have a *choice* to listen to your heart and your truest essence versus the unconscious wiring of your past. You are never your past.

So, ask yourself, are you being true to your heart—to your Loving-Trustworthy Self? Then, if you're making a choice because you feel it's the right thing to do for YOU, you're choosing powerfully and as an adult, you're owning it. No excuses, no defenses, no apologies.

Choose for yourself and finally set a course to create your own amazing destiny.

EXERCISE:

Is This Choice from the

Hurt-Wounded Self or the Loving-Trustworthy Self?

Family. School. Religion. Culture. Society. Friends. Among all the influences in our lives, it can feel tricky to parse out what our truest selves feel and want. But owning your choices and knowing they are *your conscious* (versus unconscious) choices, and that they reflect who you are now and who you want to evolve into is a fantastically POWERFUL way to live. Refer to these questions often as you begin to practice choosing from the heart of your Loving-Trustworthy Self instead of the old Hurt-Wounded Self. There are no right or wrong answers in this exercise. It's merely a guide to help you determine where your choices are coming from—a loving-trusted place or a hurt-wounded place. Once we become aware of our patterns, we begin to choose differently.

- Am I saying no to my own happiness just to make someone else happy?

- Am I trying to control or manipulate a person or an outcome?

- Is there some fear about how I will look and what others may think of me (i.e., rejection)?

  Hint: If you're making a specific choice because you're afraid of how it might make you look otherwise, then your choice is to *look* a certain way versus stand for and have what you really want.

- Am I choosing this to validate my self-worth, or to show that I'm right or smart?

- Is it to prove that I'm a good person?

- Am I afraid of being judged?

  Hint: This habit of constantly proving yourself to others is damn exhausting! I ask you to consider: does that pattern really (or ever) make you happy?

- What feelings am I having right now that are driving this choice?

- What influences am I putting ahead of my own wisdom and voice?

- What are all the choices on the table?

- What do I value and believe about this choice over another?

- Who will I show up as in the world if I make a certain choice?

- What's the impact of this choice on where I want to be in *my life* and *who I really am?*

CHAPTER 14

Ask for Help & Self-Care-ify

"From what I've seen, it isn't so much the act of asking that paralyzes us—it's what lies beneath: the fear of being vulnerable, the fear of rejection, the fear of looking needy or weak. The fear of being seen as a burdensome member of the community instead of a productive one. It points, fundamentally, to our separation from one another."

– Amanda Palmer, *The Art of Asking*

All of us need help along this journey of Life. But failing to ask for help when we need it most will only keep us isolated, anxious, unhappy. There's a reason that a lone wolf in the wild can't survive as long on his own. That's because it takes the unity of the pack to hunt together successfully; to protect any sick or injured wolf from other predators; and to exist in a connected, cooperative way. In other words, wolves teach us that mutual support and interdependence are part of nature, and essential to our survival.

Yes, the trauma of the past can trick us into thinking that the lone-wolf way is the only way for us. Growing up, we were conditioned to believe that no one really cared about us or had our backs.

Many survivors of abuse have this overblown sense of responsibility, believing they must do everything themselves, and that they're the only ones they can count on.

We had to carry the weight of this unbearable burden on such small shoulders. We were brainwashed into believing that we were responsible for everything. So, in a desperate attempt to gain some sense of control over the nightmare we were living, we put our heads down and built a wall around our hearts. As children, trying to stay in control of everything and everyone was the only way we could handle and survive the abuse. But as an adult? That kind of strategy doesn't work anymore!

Our society has grown increasingly isolated, in disconnect mode, with an alarming rise in suicides (mostly among men), notes relationship expert and bestselling author Jordan Gray. He writes, "The lone wolf may feel like asking others for support is unnecessary, unfair, weak, pathetic, or dependent." Gray adds that this resistance to asking for help and connecting in a vulnerable way with others often has deep roots in our past—"a childhood survival mechanism that served them at a time when it made sense . . . but they are unwilling to let go of it because their ego fears its own collapse."

Asking for help takes courage, even if parts of society still don't get that this is a healthy thing to do. You know when you need help, and yet, you may find yourself hesitating. But that's exactly when it's time to do some serious self-reflection, to examine why you continue to suffer, alone. Flip this help thing on its head, and ask yourself, "If I had a close friend who needed my help, wouldn't I want to know about it?" I'll bet you'd jump right in with all the support, empathy, and unconditional love you could muster. You'd just want to be there for that person and let her or him know: hey, you're *not* alone. Sometimes that's all it takes. Someone to listen, be with our pain—and us.

In my own case, I resisted asking for help for too many years. During the course of therapy and healing, I finally began to see how I'd accumulated this misperception of what "help" means. Instead of shutting down and judging myself, I started to follow the thread of curiosity. *Why did I feel this way? Why am I so reluctant to ask for help?* And then, eventually, I traced it back to those chronic, victim beliefs of shame, guilt, and worthlessness.

Ironically, I had the toughest time asking for help whenever I was feeling the most depressed, hopeless, and really crappy about myself. My thoughts would race, *Oh, this isn't that important* (I'm not important), or *I'll just be bothering them* (I'm not worth it), or *I should know this already* (I'm stupid), or *If I ask anyone I'll look needy and weak* (I am needy and weak). You can likely relate and fill in your own negative thoughts here.

Once I started to see that all those false judgments and excuses came from old childhood wounds, I started to shift my perspective. I started to tell those mean and nasty gremlins in my head, "Thanks for your input, guys, but I can't do this alone. None of us can."

Make that leap to ask for help. Also, pay attention to that person's reaction. Were you supported and loved unconditionally, or was there a negative reaction that made you scurry back into your shell? It's crucial to know whom you can be vulnerable with, and whom you can depend on for support. Sometimes, even our closest circle of family and friends let us down. On the other hand, they can also surprise us, leaving us wondering why we were so afraid to ask in the first place. Recognizing that there are people in your life who are simply unavailable emotionally, or who only reinforce your negative misperceptions, is a key part of your own healing.

> *You build your emotional toolbox by*
> *knowing thyself—and knowing others.*
> *In other words, don't go to those*
> *who aren't capable of being there for you.*

Reach out and share with those who want and know how to help. (For help on knowing who to ask, check out my *Identifying Family Feelings/Triggers* exercise in the chapter, "The Family You Had vs. The Family You Create.")

SELF-CARE ISN'T AN OPTION; IT'S A MUST

I've been guilty of not taking good care of myself, often using the excuses of "too-busy, too-much-to-do!" For many years, I'd been running on overdrive, ignoring my lack of sleep, lack of exercise, horrible diet, and giving my time to everyone else—but me. I finally started to get this "self-care" thing about ten years ago (well, better late than never, as they say).

Taking time for yourself, to care for your mind, body, spirit is necessary, especially if you're a survivor of sexual abuse (or any type of abuse, for that matter). I started to schedule vacations alone and experienced some amazing places and cultures. I made that "me" time a priority and found I could refill the well best whenever I was in nature. Through meditation, I learned how important it was to connect with Spirit and the Universal collective (or God, or whatever feels right for you). I practiced being open to different kinds of experiences and people, without judgment, and wow—in the process, rediscovered a whole new, wonderful "me."

Investing in doing things that I loved, that filled my well, actually boosted my healing process exponentially (kind of like compound interest for the body, mind, soul). Taking care of yourself, dear one, isn't a luxury; it's a freakin' necessity!

GIVE YOURSELF ME-TIME PERMISSION, 'CUZ BABY, NO ONE ELSE WILL

Ever feel like you need to ask permission to be happy? To take care of yourself? To focus on what YOU really want and need?

Several years ago, as I was watching the sailboats glide in and out of the marina, the sun trying to crack through the haze, I saw a group of birds flocking around nearby empty tables searching for any morsel they could find. No one else was around. It was so peaceful. But soon it would be bustling with people, adults and children alike, taking advantage of a beautiful weekend at the ocean.

"Yes, I'm not working today," I journaled. "This feels nice, but kind of unsettling. Even the birds are working to forage some food."

Now unless you know me personally, you do *not* know how hard it is for me to just relax—and not be doing *something*. Sometimes I felt like that jazzed-up energizer bunny! If I had enough battery power, I could go nonstop. I used to feel like I *had* to be doing something at all times, even on the weekends. And, a part of me knew this wasn't necessarily good or healthy.

One day, I sat down and had a serious talk—with myself. I had been running myself into the ground, so damn busy with work certifications, trainings, conferences, relationship time, and on and on—but guess what? I'd left zero time for myself.

Like many survivors of childhood abuse, I realized: I had unwittingly fallen into the trap of, "If I only work hard enough, I will someday be successful enough, loved enough, valued enough." This constant busyness, doing, performing, proving, trying, pleasing—whew!

> *These are all compulsive symptoms that we*
> *have to do something, as much as we can*
> *possibly cram into each day and night—*
> *to feel alive, worthy, loved. Essentially,*
> *to prove that we're MORE than we think we are.*

What if you gave yourself the green light to take care of yourself; focus on what you really want; and allow for just some "being/do nothing" time, without an agenda?

In the wise goddess words of bestselling author and inspiring entrepreneur Danielle LaPorte, "If you believe that you are a child of the universe, or a product of Love, and/or a global citizen, then it's common sense that you care well for yourself. In fact, you're honor bound to love yourself . . . self-care is a divine responsibility."

So, take a close-up and personal look at the expectations and pressures you're putting yourself through—and *why*. What's your true intention behind all the busyness? What's important to you? And what's just a cover-up for feeling less-than? We're often our harshest critics and slave drivers, especially when it comes to unrealistic expectations of how we look and what others think of us. I ask myself, *Veronica, where are these "shoulds" all coming from? What if you gave yourself permission to experience something that isn't another damn "should?"*

My pursuits and passions, while very diverse, have allowed me to achieve many of my dream projects and experience an inspired, passionate life. I frequently pause, however, to reevaluate where I'm putting my focus and energy. *Is this what I want to accomplish and create?* If it's yes, then I freely give myself permission to go for it. Regular self-reflection on *why* I'm doing what I'm doing has served me well.

Don't let anything or anyone get in your way. Not even *you*.

TIPS:
Ways to Reach Out & Reach Inward for Healing

In the silence of your mind and the repetition of small, yet healthy habits, you'll find more inner peace, mental clarity, emotional strength and resilience, and an overall well-being. You'll start to walk taller and speak your truth, in a loving, nonjudgmental way. Not all self-care habits are for everyone. If something doesn't lift you up, then find what works for you. Here are some ways you can reach out for support, while reaching inward for your own healing and happiness. Absolutely, jot down your own ideas here. These are just a primer.

- Start eating healthier and drinking more water
- Schedule regular exercising and stretching (if you don't like the idea of exercise, start walking; walking is a vastly underestimated exercise)
- Practice being present in your body via yoga or breathing techniques
- Connect to Spirit through meditation, and walks in nature
- Ask for help from supportive friends and family
- Reach out to crisis help lines and a therapist if you're in crisis mode
- Search for websites and blogs that provide support and encouragement
- Listen and acknowledge your feelings and scribble them in a notebook
- Recognize your old, negative childhood beliefs, the ones you've dragged into your present life; then practice letting them go and replace them with healthier self-talks
- Share your pain and vulnerability only with the people you've found safe to share with, and don't share with those who aren't capable

- Schedule fun and leisure time like you schedule work and errands
- Release abusive, toxic people in your life

PART

3

The Power
That Is Yours

CHAPTER

15

Live for Now, Not the Past

"Stop acting as if life is a rehearsal.
Live this day as if it were your last.

The past is over and gone.
The future is not guaranteed."

– Wayne Dyer

There never seems to be enough time in the day (or night) to accomplish what you want. And, the phrase "time is an illusion" just frustrates the heck out of me because it really isn't. Time is the same for all of us—and it is finite. Whenever I miss a meeting or deadline or see another wrinkle in the mirror (reflecting back to me the wisdom of my years), I have no illusions about time. Time is real. But our thoughts about time can make us crazy, if we don't learn how to manage our mind. Too much thinking about yesterday or tomorrow just makes it worse. And remember, most of us have about 60,000 thoughts per day, mostly negative and a variation of the same darn thing.

Buddhists call this mental phenomenon the "Monkey Mind." As the Buddha himself put it, "Just as a monkey swinging through the trees grabs one branch and lets it go only to seize another, so too, that which is called thought, mind or consciousness arises and disappears continually both day and night." Yikes. All that mental swinging from branch to branch, tree to tree, makes it tough to stay in the present and focus on where you are now. Now, you can't lock up that excitable, chattering monkey—but you can learn to tame him—through practices such as meditation, yoga, tai chi, and even physical exercise.

I think the key to feeling like you have a handle on time is to live for and in the moment. There have been many books written about "living in the now," but what it really boils down to is focusing on what you can do—and what you have—*today*. None of us knows what will happen down the road, nor can we change what's happened in the rearview mirror. Training our mind to live for today helps alleviate unnecessary stress and anxiety whenever we think about what might happen next. The anxiety and stress of thinking about past experiences gone bad or what needs to happen for us to have a happier future is exhausting and can even shut us down completely.

Right now, take a situation or relationship that you're anxious about and imagine it in a different place, a place of "no time." Yes, I know I said time is real—and it is. But nothing changes for the better if we get all sped up or worried about it, does it? Often, our anxiety has mostly to do with the past—and we project that past into the future. Now, that's an illusion, one that can really sabotage our happiness, growth, and success.

Remember each moment in your mind is just that. *A moment in time.* Consider this: How much could you accomplish if you didn't overthink or fret about what might happen tomorrow or what happened yesterday? You cannot live in the past nor can you live in the future. Don't allow a past pain to run your mind (or your life). Painful events from the past are only memories— not a predictor of your future. Try to recognize the very moment you're assigning past experiences or future expectations to your actions and reactions. Clear the slate of your mind. Use your present knowledge to propel you forward with greater confidence and enhanced self-awareness *knowing* that you can handle any situation. Because you can.

Interesting to notice that the moment we decide something and act on it, it's no longer the present—it becomes the past. Whatever you're experiencing in this moment, you're experiencing right now, or it's not truly an experience. Yes, we can recall a past experience, and we can imagine the future. But when it comes to "time," neither are real. We certainly don't experience the future—we only have anxiety or imaginings about what the future may bring—and often think our thoughts are real. Whoa, what a mind game that is!

> *How fascinating that a moment can be*
> *filled with so many emotions from our past*
> *that we project into our future—to the point*
> *that we let these past and future*
> *thoughts stand in our way of* **living now.**

One way I keep the "not enough time" hounds at bay is to take action. I make my plans or lists, check a few things off, then get distracted and start making more lists. Ha. The lists, however, don't mean anything until I act on them. Action is always fulfilling because it gets things done and brings you one step closer to fulfilling your goals and dreams. Even if you experience some sense of failure after you take action, at least you'll experience the result of that action, positive or negative, and gain insight and feedback on how to do things differently. But, at least, you'll still be moving in the right direction.

As a goal-oriented, overachieving, in-control kind of woman, just "allowing" myself to feel "satisfaction with action" helps keep me grounded in the present. Sometimes you just have to give yourself a break and allow "time" to pass.

You chill out, regroup, and take some time to revive before taking any action.

My morning mantra is: "Things will happen in their own time, Veronica. People will show up in the right time, and you will have enough time. Trust."

> *Be aware: whenever your mind wanders*
> *down that self-sabotaging path of "not enough"*
> *or any other negative judgment that projects the*
> *picture of the past into your future, it's only*
> *an anxiety builder and, frankly, an action killer.*

So, as you learn and grow, be kinder and more compassionate to yourself. Start training yourself to allow for the now, and trust you have enough time. Because, in the end, that's all we can do.

Don't miss your present—the gift of life that's only your today—by living in the past or dwelling on the future.

TIPS:
It takes practice to stay mindful of our thoughts and see them for what they are: just thoughts.

Here are some tips to help you stay focused in the present moment.

- *Practice breathing.*

  This might sound obvious but many of us aren't taught how to breathe properly—in a way that relaxes us and reduces stress. In fact, we often unconsciously hold our breath whenever we're tense. Over the years, we can drift into this harmful habit of shallow chest breathing, which tightens the muscles, leading to neck pain and headaches, and even panic attacks. There are many methods and teachers out there (just Google "breathing techniques" and find one that resonates). I also urge you to meditate; starting at 3 minutes a day, and build up from there. Try this simple method: breathe in slowly through your nose to a count of 7, hold it for 5 seconds, and then exhale slowly through the mouth for 7 seconds. Do this several times and notice how your chest starts to open and your whole body gradually unwinds, becomes more at peace. Breathing techniques and meditation will ground and center you. Experiment with different methods to gently pull you out of that Monkey Mind zone.

- *Get your grateful on.*

  There's a wise saying, "If you can't be thankful for what you receive, be thankful for what you escape." That doesn't mean you don't want more out of life (of course you do!). But studies show that gratitude (versus self-pity) yields multiple health benefits for us: builds mental resilience, boosts self-esteem, improves sleep, increases empathy and lowers aggression, reduces depression, and helps build healthier relationships. Wow! So why not be thankful for what you have (and are)? Why not bring your awareness inward and appreciate all you have right now? Every day, morning or night, jot down 5 things you're grateful for (it's often the things we take for granted: pets, home, friends, healthy, sense of humor, etc.). It's important to have future goals, but it's just as important to appreciate the journey and where you are.

- *Notice the Monkey Mind without judging it.*
  When the negative chatter of the Monkey Mind (or, as I call mine, "Fred in the Head") negative chatter swings through your brain (as it will), practice noticing it without reacting or taking it too seriously. Ask yourself, *Is this thought coming from a negative past experience or my fear of a negative future experience?* Notice how those negative thoughts make you feel and then make a conscious choice to decide if it's even worth acting on—otherwise, thank that monkey and let it go on its merry way through the jungle. Trust yourself first.

- *Focus your priorities.*
  We humans have a habit of stacking all our problems, concerns, and must-dos—until the pile grows as a high as that crazy beanstalk tree that Jack climbed up into the sky. *Oh my God!* we think as we tumble into a pit of over-whelm. *There's not enough time to do all of this!* Stephen R. Covey in *7 Habits of Highly Effective People* offered a super simple approach to help us: sort your to-dos across four rankings: *important/not important* and *urgent/not urgent.* Make your list and be honest about where your tasks and goals fall. Anything urgent *and* important is your top priority. Whatever is not important or not urgent

drops to the bottom (and may have to fall off completely), with everything else in the middle. Also, get realistic: you're never going to finish everything on that list. *Ever.* As long as you're breathing, there'll always be "things to do." So "eat the frog" as they say and tackle the harder things first (break it up into smaller steps, one action at a time—because you're not going to pay off all your debt in one day or write that novel in a week!). Immerse yourself with smaller actions on those big-time goals, and you'll get there. Remember, trust the process and stay curious about the journey—one step, one breath, one moment at a time.

CHAPTER 16

Connect in Your Own Way to Spirit

"Spirituality can release blocks, lead you to ideas, and make your life artful. Sometimes when we pray for guidance, we're guided in unexpected directions. We may want a lofty answer and we get the intuition to clean our bedroom. It can seem so humble and picky and that you don't necessarily think of it as spiritual guidance."

– Julia Cameron

As I sat on the edge of the Grand Canyon, the fresh snow glistened upon the red-orange rocks of the cliff's spine-tingling drop-off. The snow had stopped falling a few hours ago. The clouds, lighter from the release, floated like huge blankets of cotton in the sky, throwing eerie shadows over the canyon, including every living and nonliving thing that existed. The brisk wind whipped effortlessly across the five-thousand-foot-deep gorge, as if to say, "I can go wherever I please, over cliffs, through trees, and down all the steep ravines." The wind didn't care that the walls and cliffs were a mile deep, as it wound its way to the very bottom and back up again, sometimes with such force that it knocked down wobbly signs and old, fragile tree trunks, leaving snakes and other critters a bit shaken, but alive.

What a magnificent place this is, I thought. I felt small and insignificant compared to the astonishing beauty of this immense canyon, formed millions of years ago by mother earth herself. As I lingered here, I noticed that my worries, doubts, and any negativity strangely melted away. All I could sense in that moment was Pure Love. I felt a deep affinity for this place and its mysteries, for the people around me, and for myself. I was in awe of the world, of nature, and everyone who lived, past and present.

Have you ever had such an inexplicable, spiritual experience? I hope so because such a profound otherworldly connection is the best medicine for a weary soul.

We all crave connection and a sense of belonging and often feel an inexplicable connection to things and places, music and art, animals and nature. But most fulfilling of all is the connection we feel to others. Every person on this planet has his or her own way of connecting to something beyond themselves, to what I and others call Spirit (or God, or the Universe, and so on). You may believe in an Eastern or Western religion, or perhaps you feel drawn to New Age philosophies, including eclectic, metaphysical practices such as crystals, channeling, visualization, and finding enlightenment in nature. We should have tolerance for all these beliefs; none of us holds the golden key to spiritual Truth.

I believe that neither religion nor any type of spirituality should be forced upon anyone; spirituality is a deeply personal experience. An experience that draws us closer to the realization: we're all a part of something much bigger.

Spirituality, for me, is about recognizing and celebrating that we are all inextricably linked to each other by a mystical Power far greater than us, and that the energies of Love and Compassion are foundational to this spiritual Power.

For me, nature has a way of inspiring this connection, that curious feeling of belonging and wonderment, a portal of Universal truth about our creation and existence. Nature itself has been a major source of healing for me.

Raised as Roman Catholic, I once seriously contemplated becoming a nun, right about the time that the abuse started. I can still recall the image from my catechism teachings of God holding his scepter, sitting in a throne-like chair, the world at his feet. When I was young, that's how I once thought of God, an omnipotent being who loved us, but also looked down on us, judged and punished us if we ever dared to cross him. In the religious teachings of my childhood, there was a whole lot of talk about fire and brimstone (much like my father!). When the abuse started happening, there was a lot of internal questioning for me. *Why was this happening? What did I do to deserve this? God, why did you abandon me?* Because it felt like God didn't care and had turned his back on my suffering. I had been a good and decent child, and a devout Christian. This feeling of being abandoned by God played deeply into the belief that "I must have done something to deserve this." Ultimately, it left me grasping for a different kind of spirituality, one where I could feel connected, not separate. *What is the truth of the world? Who am I? Is God even real?*

Well, I got my answers during two unexpected out-of-body experiences.

The first time was when I was going through the most difficult part of psychotherapy. I had been working on letting go of feeling at fault for losing the connection to my family, the one I thought I had protected by staying silent and obedient. I felt utterly alone, adrift, and frightened. I needed to feel loved, to know that I mattered, and that I belonged—somewhere!

I was sitting on my favorite park bench in Laguna Beach, a seaside southern California town known for its artist community, rocky bluffs, and sandy beaches. The bench sits underneath a flag pole on a cliff that overlooks the Pacific Ocean. You can see the beach from both directions and for many years, I've lovingly referred to it as "My Bench."

Back then, I had just started to practice meditation, so I closed my eyes and began to breathe slowly, deeply. Aware of the crashing waves and cool, fresh air, I tried to empty my mind of thoughts. As each thought appeared, I'd allow the feeling that came with it, then with my next breath, release it. I did this for about five minutes and began to feel lighter. Until I heard the roar of a speeding Jet Ski directly in front of me but still a ways out. At that moment, I thought, *Ow, that hurts!* The Jet Ski continued its race, bouncing up and down across the waves. It felt like a knife dragging across my skin. *Get off me!* I thought, and then it hit me: *I was the ocean*—and could feel what it was feeling.

I opened my eyes. All the flowers, the ocean itself, the beach, the clouds in the sky suddenly looked more brilliant and, the strange thing is, I felt like *I was part of all of it.* I instantly knew that I belonged. The breathtaking beauty of the scenery, the rhythm of the ocean, and the power of nature was stunning. A sense of peace, inspiration, and security washed over me. I felt in my bones that there was a supreme, loving energy that created all things.

I was part of the *love* and *design* of the Universe and there was no longer any need to seek validation from anyone, or a desire to prove my worth. I felt that we all were coexisting in this space and energy of time.

It was indescribable. *I belong. I am loved.* My eyes filled with joyful tears, and my heart burst open with a feeling of infinite connection. It's a feeling that I try to recreate each time I meditate.

My second out-of-body experienced happened at a time when I was studying the Eastern religions and feeling a stronger connection to their philosophies, specifically, Buddhism and Taoism. Eastern religions gave me that sense I was seeking: a deeper connection to the Universe that was already inside me versus outside me (remember, I grew up believing that God was outside of us, not inside or a part of us).

I had just learned about a simple meditative chant, "I have a body." The chant's intent is to help you understand that you are *more* than your physical body. You are also a spirit, an essence of unconditional love. I was driving home after a singing rehearsal, and started to chant, "I have a body . . . I have a body . . . I have a body." After about ten minutes or so, I began to feel lighter. I looked down at my hands on the steering wheel and realized that I couldn't feel it or my hands! I glanced to my right at the side of the freeway and noticed shiny ivy vines climbing the embankment. Except the image I saw was what they call in photography, a negative image—meaning the brighter, lighter portions appeared dark and the dark portions appeared light. Suddenly, I found myself floating over the ivy vines, and then in the next instant, I was the ivy plant! It all happened so fast and instantaneous. And again, I realized: *I'm not alone, I'm a part of everything, and part of the energy of everything.* We, all species, humans and plants and animals, are all One, collectively. Next, I was the concrete bridge and peered down to see my own car moving under the overpass.

Whoa, I have to get back in my body, I thought, a bit panicked now. I wriggled and shook my hands until I could finally feel the wheel again. Mind you, all of this happened in the space of about fifteen seconds. Ahem, I now know it was a mistake to do this kind of chanting while driving! I don't recommend it.

This second out-of-body experience again reminded me that we are all connected. That there *is* a universal connection to everything and everyone. The utter love, peace, and connection I felt had opened my heart to an inner knowing (not faith), but a real *knowing* that there was way more to life than I had once thought. That Spirit, or God, or the Universe, was very real.

I was comforted in knowing that I wasn't alone anymore—and never had been. I didn't need anything outside me to feel this spiritual connection.

It's not uncommon for trauma survivors to "leave their bodies" and disassociate from what's happening as a way of self-protection. Survivors may have trouble feeling grounded in their body whenever faced with a crisis, major change, or challenge. Of course, I wonder if I was able to reach this out-of-body state more easily because I had done so in my younger years whenever I was being abused. It's important, however, to practice feeling and respecting your own body, to acknowledge the feelings you have around the post-traumatic stress. The more grounded you become, the easier it gets to accept emotions, then release them. You'll also grow increasingly confident that you can handle any challenges as they arise.

EXERCISE:
Create Your Own Spiritual Support Lines

I've learned to welcome any challenge that comes my way because I've shifted my mindset to see a challenge as an opportunity for my personal growth. A chance to demonstrate who I really am, as well as a way to reflect on my choices and actions, and how they impact others and myself. Facing challenging situations is also a good time to reevaluate what's most important in your life, and what's worthy of your time and energy—and what's not.

If dealing with any stressful situation leaves you feeling drained and hinders you from being yourself, maybe it's time to examine your part in it. Do you want to keep living with that person? Working in that field? Spending time with those friends? If you choose to continue to engage with this challenge, whatever it is, then you must start taking care of yourself in ways that lessen the stress, fatigue, anger, depression, etc. Ask yourself: *Where can I go for support, strength, courage, and unconditional love?*

My go-to spiritual support line is my connection to nature. Whenever I'm feeling especially stressed, I know it's time to "make time" to head to the beach or take a walk among nature. For me personally, reconnecting to Spirit is much easier in natural surroundings. I can hear the wise voice of Spirit more clearly once I'm away from the nonstop barrage of electronics and people talking. The rhythms of the ocean waves, the splashes of a waterfall, or the whispers of the wind in a tree-filled forest call out to me to remember: I have a deeper connection to a higher power, even when I forget. It's also a total recharge for my mind, body, and soul.

I urge you to explore different ways you can reconnect to Spirit (or God, the Universe), and hear the wisdom of your own inner guides. Here are some ideas to prime the pump.

1. **Enjoy Music.** Play an instrument, sing, or put on your favorite songs.

2. **Paint.** A physical art, any style of painting can release painful emotions and help you reconnect to your truest self as well as a higher power.

3. **Embrace Nature.** Any time spent outdoors, in nature, can relax and help you regain your focus and what's really important to you, not to mention reconnect you to something bigger than yourself.

4. **Exercise.** Yoga, tai chi, bicycling, running, walking, dancing, etc., all these types of exercise will help ground you in your body and pull you out of the Monkey Mind chatter.

5. **Meditate.** The practice of meditation is no longer for the monks. Executives, homemakers, and even children are learning the benefits of meditation, and how it helps us mange our emotions and feel a deeper connection with the Universe.

6. **Free-Form Write.** Free-form writing is a technique where you start writing continuously whatever pops up in your head. It doesn't have to make sense and can jump from thought to thought. Free-form writing helps to clear out the cobwebs and can often release painful, buried emotions and help you rediscover a deeper connection with Spirit and yourself. Use a pad of paper and pen (not the computer), and light a candle near you.

7. **Self-Care.** Too often we put ourselves last. But it's vital for you to fill the well (or the well runs dry!). Take a warm bath, try aromatherapy at your desk, get a facial, book a massage. Whatever you can do to open your senses and relax will help you reconnect.

Remember: finding a spiritual connection is different for everyone. There is no right way. Walk your own path. Start today, from where you are. Be wary of anyone who claims his or her way is the only way. This is your journey, not mine or anyone else's.

CHAPTER 17

Live Your Best Life

*"I survived because the fire inside me
burned brighter than the fire around me."*

– Joshua Graham

Once you discover what's behind the fear, what parts of your life are incongruent with your own beliefs and values, and where you struggle the most whenever you're feeling out of control, invisible, or unworthy—you'll never turn back to the old, self-defeating ways. Whenever you bring the unseen of your psyche into the Light, and reveal it for what it is, you can't help but respond (not react), choose, and take action from the core of who you really are.

> *The aftereffects of childhood abuse often
> impact nearly every area of one's life. The
> only way to get to the other side of the pain is
> to pull back the curtain and reveal what
> or who is pulling the strings inside you.*

Strong feelings are part of the healing process. Don't be afraid or deny them. Your pain, confusion, and frustration will recede with time as you work on finding your way back.

It can be difficult to heal in isolation. Silence and secrecy only perpetuate our loneliness and reinforce isolation. We once dealt with the pain in our heads, separate from others, or withdrew completely by numbing out with addictions, or denying our feelings. If you want your healing journey to move quicker, then you must seek support and understanding from outside yourself.

It's never easy to remain positive when negativity surrounds us, and you'll need a steady diet of reminders. I've adopted simple, yet powerful beliefs, to remind me. As Zig Ziglar, one of the greatest motivational authors and speakers of all time, once said, "People often say that motivation doesn't last. Well, neither does bathing— that's why we recommend it daily."

I leave you with twenty beliefs I turn to whenever you need to wash away the negativity. Prior to my own journey of self-discovery and healing of my body, soul, and psyche, many of these beliefs were contrary to how I had viewed the world. These beliefs have helped free me from the grips of pessimism and cynicism. Feel free to copy any of them and post where you can see them. Or, create your own!

20 POWERFUL BELIEFS

1. **Feeling stuck is a sign that it's time to make a change.**
   When we're unhappy and feeling like there's no way out, we can feel overwhelmed and become paralyzed. We lose faith and beat up ourselves for not being able to do whatever we need to do to grow and feel more fulfilled. Whenever you're feeling this way, know that it's time to

take action, to make a change in how you're behaving and communicating with yourself and others.

2. **What other people think about me is their issue, not mine.** Don't take on other people's negative energy and don't take it personally. Most pessimists are negative with everyone, not just you. What they say and do is a projection of their own narrow-minded reality. Even when a situation seems personal, even if someone insults you directly, it often has nothing to do with you. What others say and do, and the opinions they have, are based entirely on their own self-reflection. So, let that shit go.

3. **I'm free to be 100 percent totally me, my True Self.** Can you remember who you were—before the world told you who you should be? Happiness is found when you stop comparing yourself to everyone else and what they want. Stop living for other people and their opinions. Be true to yourself. Don't abandon what you want and need or how you feel. You're the only person in charge of your life. Conversely, don't force your expectations on how you think everyone else should behave. Because not everyone has lived your experiences or views the world like you do. If you expect that everyone should do as "I do," you'll be forever disappointed.

4. **I don't have to have it all figured out to gain momentum.** Sometimes we wear the perfectionist mask, always trying to be so perfect to prove we're good enough, smart enough, etc. In order to move forward, you just need to have faith, a knowing, and then jump into the unknown. Because, ultimately, all decisions lack sufficient information.

5. **Even the smallest step toward change is progress.**
When you take any action toward change, or your goals,
it's always better than no action. You'll always learn from
your actions—because any action, no matter how small, is
progress.

6. **Life isn't perfect, but it sure feels great to be alive.**
Our goal is never about creating the perfect life, but to live
an imperfect life from curiosity, love, and excitement. Get
up every morning and take a good look around you. Take
nothing for granted. Everything truly is extraordinary.
Every day, a gift. Never treat life so casually. Be amazed in
every way.

7. **It's OK to have down days.** Expecting life to be wonderful all the time is like expecting to swim in an ocean in
which waves only rise and never fall. The rising and falling
waves are part of the ocean, and so it is with Life. Let go
and find peace with the reality of the ups and downs. Don't
let the downtimes drag you down.

8. **Even when I'm struggling, there's so much to be
grateful for.** We tend to forget that happiness doesn't
come as a result of getting something we don't have, but in
appreciating everything we do have. Stress thrives when
your worry list grows longer than your gratitude list.
Happiness thrives when your gratitude list grows longer
than your worry list. So, get your grateful on now.

9. **Every experience is just another lesson.** Disappointments and failure are two of the surest stepping stones to
success and fulfillment. So don't let a hard lesson harden

your heart. When things go wrong, learn what you can and then push the tragic thinking and mistakes aside. Remember, life's best lessons are often learned at the worst times, from the worst mistakes. We must fail in order to know and hurt in order to grow. Good things often fall apart so better things can fall together in their place.

10. **Nothing changes if nothing changes.** If we don't like our current situation, *do* something about it. There's an old saying that the definition of crazy is doing the same thing over and over again and expecting a different result. Do something different today.

11. **Not everything is meant to stay.** Change can be terrifying, yet all positive growth and healing requires the call to change. Sometimes you have to find the good in goodbye, even when your heart is still breaking. Because the past is a place of reference, not a place of residence. Be strong when everything seems to be going wrong, keep taking those small steps, and eventually you'll find what you're looking for. Learn to trust your own journey, even when you don't understand it.

12. **Being wrong is the first step to being right.** Sometimes the wrong choices bring us to the right places. To be creative, resourceful, and productive in life, you must first lose your fear of being wrong. And remember, a fear like this can only survive inside you if you let it live there.

13. **I don't need to hold onto what's holding me back.** You're not what has happened to you in the past; you are what you choose to become in the present. It's time to toss

out the old beliefs and routines that are holding you back. Respect yourself enough to walk away from anything that no longer grows you. Listen to your intuition, not your ego or the voices of others. When you stop chasing the wrong beliefs, you give the right ones a chance to catch you.

14. **My happiness today is the result of my thoughts.** Happiness starts with you—not your relationships, your job, or your money. But with you. It's not always easy to find happiness within, but it's impossible to find it outside of us. Regardless of the situation you face, the attitude you choose is what matters most. Remember, you can't have a positive life with a negative attitude. When negativity controls your thoughts, it stunts your growth and opportunities. If you realize how powerful your thoughts are, you'd do your best to never think another negative thought again, or at least let it float past instead of hanging onto it.

15. **New beginnings can feel like endings.** Whenever we release something or someone that's been a part of our life for some time, it can feel like an unbearably painful ending. But also look for the silver lining. Stay strong and look forward to new challenges, people, and places. Grieve as long as you need to. Then, get back in the game of your Life.

16. **Who I spend time with matters.** Surround yourself with people who love and lift you higher. Hang with the greats—those who see the greatest potential in you, even when you don't see it in yourself. Spend time with high-

vibration people who share your love of life and aren't dragging you down or judging you.

17. **Drama and judgments are a total waste.** Make a promise to yourself to stop the unnecessary egoic drama before it begins, to breathe deeply and peacefully, and to love others and yourself without conditions. Promise to laugh at your own mistakes and to realize no one is perfect; we're all human. Feelings of self-worth can flourish only when individual differences are appreciated, mistakes are tolerated, communication is open, and rules are flexible.

18. **People are judging me far less than I think.** The truth is, while you're busy worrying about what others think of you, they're busy worrying about what you think of them. Ha. The good news is this knowledge instantly frees you to let loose and do more of what you want. You'll also liberate others to do the same.

19. **The work is worth it.** Lose the expectation that everything in life should be easy. There are no shortcuts to any place worth going. Enjoy the journey and the challenge. See the value in your efforts and be patient, loving, and kind with yourself. Realize that patience isn't about waiting; it's about keeping a good attitude while being determined to live your dreams. It's knowing deep down that the work is well worth it, in the end.

20. **Trust my heart, not what others say.** When we're connected to our hearts and higher guidance, we always know what to trust. What others say or do is frankly irrelevant. You have nothing to prove to anyone. Your

job is to love and expand. Your mission is to live out an extraordinary existence.

Dear ones, my wish for you, as you navigate this wonderful and complex world, is that you know the Truth—you *are* the Love and the Light—and always have been.

> ***Always know and never forget: You are wise, strong,***
> ***and made of pure love. So, be YOU! It's time to Know***
> ***your Power and Create your Own Life.***

My Story

BORN WITH WINGS ON MY SHOULDERS

You've just read how I overcame years of childhood sexual abuse and the tools I used to reclaim my power so that I could genuinely feel valued, loved, and whole again. Now I want to share with you my *whole* story. I think you'll relate and possibly find that you've had similar thoughts and feelings.

I was raised in a nice, middle-class neighborhood in Southern California. Three boys, one girl (me). No surprise that I was a bit of a tomboy. With all that testosterone buzzing about, competition was naturally a part of our daily lives, and as the only girl, I had to pedal fast to keep up with my brothers and prove myself their equal, while silently shouting in my head, "Hey I'm not just a girl!"

Like most children, I believed that I had magical powers. I remember pedaling around on my bike, a tiny red blanket tied around my neck to let everyone know, I was Super Girl! Yes, even at age eight, I felt like I could do anything! Life was my oyster, and there were so many options for me. *I can do anything, I am loved, I am amazing, I am confident. I am Veronica.*[10]

---

10. Actually, I was born as Gerlinde but changed it many years ago. Choosing a new name for myself was part of my personal transformation; it helped me psychically leave the past behind. The name Veronica came to me in a future-self meditation. Only later did I discover it meant "true image."

Soon my world would take a dark turn, however, and my powers would quickly fade into the dark. Who and what I "thought" I was born as would sadly morph into a twisted, hollow version of myself.

MY FAMILY'S BEGINNING

My parents fell in love and married in Germany when my father was an Army sergeant during the Korean War. He'd been stationed there when he met my mother, a very young woman working in the servicemen's laundry facility. She was only eighteen when he brought her to America. She left her parents, two brothers, and seven sisters far behind. She must have truly been in love and/or extremely brave. I can't help but wonder sometimes if there wasn't something in her own family that she was escaping. But to this day, she has never told me.

Dad was a controlling man and strict disciplinarian. You know the saying, "Wait till your father gets home!" Well I heard that many times throughout my childhood. My father even had a favorite "belt" that he had made from a one-inch-thick wooden stick with two leather straps attached. I remember that punishing belt all too well and how he used it on my brothers and me. It stung like hell and left red welts across our legs and butts. We learned quickly that we never wanted to do *anything* that might bring us such punishment and pain. So, needless to say, we did our best to be perfect children. Sometimes, however, the smallest thing would set Dad off, just a wrong glance or an innocent question. My brothers and I never knew for sure if what we said or did was "good enough" to warrant his love and avoid his rage. If you want to know how to have your brain rewired so that it forgets how to be confident and secure, well, that's certainly one way that trauma can beat the life out of you. Of course, there are other ways far worse.

By the time my mother turned twenty-four she was still not accustomed to living in an unfamiliar country, on top of the stress of raising the four of us. She was submissive and obedient to my father, but as a child, I never grasped her passive, wounded nature. I now recognize that it was hard for her to leave her own home, move to a new country with a controlling man she barely knew, let alone quickly adopt the language or customs. She had zero outside support from family and friends (except the few couples that were friends of my father's). Back then, cell phones hadn't been invented yet. It was too costly to call her family in Germany, where she'd been raised and fairly sheltered in a small town there. Before immigrating to the U.S. with my father, my mother was on track to become an opera singer, studying with a voice coach in the city of Baumholder. She showed true talent and had the voice of an angel, really. Mom never realized or knew her true greatness, even if at one point in her life, she too must have felt the power of that symbolic red cape fluttering in the breeze behind her, reminding her that she could do or be anything.

We attended Catholic school from an early age because Dad felt that a Catholic education was better than public school. More opportunities, stricter discipline, and a God-given path, he said. Underneath all of that was the fact that my father had trouble reading and struggled to hide his shame around this. To his credit, he didn't want his children to ever feel that way and paid the private tuition even though it meant two jobs and grueling, long days.

THE MOMENT MY WORLD FIRST COLLAPSED

I was only twelve when I lost everything that red cape personified.

I was swimming in our backyard pool, and no one else was home except Dad, and as I scrambled out of the water and dried myself off, he flatly ordered: "Take of your bathing suit and get into bed with me." Fearful of a whipping, I did what he said. I had spent a lot of time at the convent just a block from our Catholic elementary school and was contemplating becoming a nun. *This isn't right*, I thought. *I know Daddy loves me. But this feels wrong.* Laying stark-naked in my parents' bed next to my naked father who had an erection as he pulled me to him, I took his face in my small hands. "Daddy," I trembled, "I don't like this." His face dropped. "Get up," a mix of disappointment and shame in his voice.

Afterward, I don't remember how many days, I felt so ugly and scared, that I finally, told my mother. I remember her looking a lot like I felt—lost, angry, and sad. She called my father at work and told him to come home immediately. I could hear my parents arguing in the bedroom for quite some time. Finally, they called me in and sat me on the edge of their bed, a picture of Jesus on the wall staring down at me. They both assured me, this was a mistake that Dad had made. He was sorry, it wasn't my fault, and it would never happen again.

My mother was crying, her face eroded with devastation. I wanted so much to reach out and comfort her, to take care of her, and let her know that I was OK. This tragedy was the beginning of the end for both of us—a mother and daughter's sense of safety, security, and trust—shattered.

Later that same year, my father approached me again. To this day the timing of his next attack remains fuzzy, like a nightmare in which you recall the worst parts but can't retrieve all the details. He would sneak into my room after everyone was asleep, Mom knocked out cold on tranquilizing pills. I see now that she herself was trapped with no family to turn to for help. I will never know her pain.

My mother lost herself. Her husband's controlling behavior had been hard enough on her. But now this? It must have felt as surreal to her as it was for me. Ever since I had first told her what he had done to me, her depression turned severe, and at one point, we were all gathered in the hospital waiting room while our mother underwent shock therapy treatments. They failed to help her.

Never revealing the truth to the doctors, the police, or anyone who might have helped us, the story she began telling herself was that *she* was the ill one, suffering from manic depression, and requiring prescription drugs to stay alive. She saw herself as a victim of whatever the world would throw at her. She felt utterly helpless and decided she had zero control over her life. Essentially, despair and hopelessness got the best of her. She lives out her last days that way.

I learned from my mother how the past can grip us by the throat, pulling us down with these made-up stories we tell ourselves that keep us small and a victim—that keep us from remembering our power.

Yes, dwelling on the past diminishes our true greatness and potential. It slams the door on any future happiness.

Father always told me it was my fault, and since my mother wasn't available to him sexually, that role was now mine. His attacks increased to several times a week. I cannot even describe what he did to me. At first, he was touching me like a lover would, and amped it up to oral sex. One night he dragged me out to the family camper in the front yard, just outside our house where everyone slept, but far enough that no one could hear my cries of pain.

That night he raped me. I can still smell his cheap cologne, how he sprayed it on himself to cover up the evidence. Shame, terror, and exhaustion consumed me. To this day, any whiff of that cologne triggers my memory of that brutal night. I tried to fight him, but I wasn't strong enough. I was only twelve. That night and in the years that followed, my father threatened me to keep me quiet, saying things such as, "If anyone finds out, I'll go to jail, you will all be homeless and Mom will have to be committed to the hospital again," or "You'll never see your brothers again," and one of the most bizarre ones was, "You always have to do what your Man says or he will leave you." It was complete mind control and manipulation, especially for a child who, of course, believed the parent. The incest continued for six years. During that long, dark tunnel of my life, I was so afraid someone would find out and blame *me*. Plus, he had convinced me it was up to me to protect our family. It was my fault and my responsibility to stay silent. And, that's when something clicked inside me, and I began to believe that I had to control everything and everyone, or life would actually fall apart.

That once happy, brave little girl pedaling her bike around the neighborhood, proudly wearing her homemade super-cape was gone. In her place, a different girl emerged, one filled with shame and guilt and confusion. A child who believed that it was *her* fault, and that she'd *never* be good enough for anyone. Ever.

It was a rough journey for me, to say the least, especially when I was going through puberty (and that's challenging enough under normal circumstances). I had to hide what my father was doing to me right at a time when I was becoming attracted to boys my age, bouncing back and forth like a ping-pong ball, wondering what was right and wrong, and feeling good one moment, then bad the next.

One morning, our sixth-grade class ran to the window to watch a streaker sprint across the school playground. Streaking became a fad in the early 1970s in which mostly college students would strip naked and run in public, crowded places, either as a wild dare or to protest something. I remember Sister Stephens pulling down the blinds, as she remarked to us girls, "If you're that interested, ask your brother or father to show you." I felt sick to my stomach. She had no idea how much I already knew about the male anatomy. Shame, guilt, and pain coursed through me like poison.

THE TRUTH COMES OUT

I was eighteen, had just started college and dating my soon-to-be husband. I came home to visit my parents and brothers, but Dad was the only one there. I put my purse on the kitchen counter and he immediately started digging through it. When he found my birth control pills, he lost it. You see, I was supposed to be his woman. He grabbed and dragged me into one of my brother's rooms, forced me on a sofa bed that was open and strapped me down. That was the last time my father raped me.

About a year later, I was a married woman. I still hadn't told my husband the truth. We were having some marital problems, and in a moment of desperation and anger, I confessed to him that the source of our conflicts likely stemmed from the incest. I told him how my own father had molested and raped me for years. He was stunned. I was stunned as well. I couldn't believe the dark secret that I had been keeping finally tumbled out of me.

"You've got to tell your brothers!"

"No, no! I can't tell my brothers!" You see, I was still living in this weird twilight zone place of denial. Yes, it had been horrific.

But I got through it, didn't I? Why did my brothers need to know? *I was OK, really! I learned to deal with it in my own way. Just leave it the hell alone.*

My then-husband insisted again, "No, no," he shook his head. "You've got to tell them!"

Within minutes I was on the phone with my oldest brother. When I told him the ugly truth, what he said next surprised me. "Now it all makes sense," he sighed.

The next day my husband and I were at his grandmother's house when we got a call from that same brother. He had confronted our father that day. My heart pounded, my whole body shivered. I knew there was a gun in the house and that Dad had reacted so violently to the accusation, that my mother and two brothers still living at home had fled to a local hotel.

I have to do something, I thought. *I have to take care of Dad.* So, I called him at the house.

"Hello?" a gruff, stern voice answered.

"Dad?" I squeaked.

Through the phone, I could hear his rabid, uncontrollable breathing and sobbing, coated with intense rage.

"I'm sorry, I'm sorry Dad." I quickly hung up, imagining him slithering his way through the phone, grabbing me by the throat and killing me on the spot. I still couldn't believe the psychological hold he had on me. *What? For God's sake! I just told him that I'm sorry?*

My husband and I arranged to have the police patrol past our house for a week; I was that terrified. By the end of that week, my father was admitted to the hospital on a psychiatric hold.

MY POWERS BEGIN TO REEMERGE

This was the beginning of the end of our family, the one I thought I had somehow managed to protect by staying silent. But for me? This was the beginning of a new life, one in which once the truth had come out, I could begin to reclaim parts of me I had long lost: my courage and strength and enthusiasm that the little girl inside me once knew. Yes, my road to healing was long. But the powers of confidence, forgiveness, fulfillment, and unconditional love were well worth it.

I'm at a different place now, where, believe it or not, whenever I recall those horrible days, I now feel a sense of power. My true story has finally surfaced. I was never a bad child. I was a scared and traumatized little girl who did the best she could to survive. I have dug deep into my soul and psyche to untangle and uncover all the lies and false judgments about myself.

I'm at peace with the past and happy in the present. I live a very full, exciting life, brimming with creativity, fun, and love. I feel extremely grateful for every wonderful day on this planet. Dear ones, I wish the same for you.

Never forget:

You are beautiful, wise and unique; and your youthful spirit is in your passions. You are Loved.

So . . . Remember and Know Your Power.

Resources

Adult Survivors of Child Abuse

http://www.ascasupport.org

Resources and recovery program

Darkness to Light

https://www.d2l.org/

1-866-FOR-LIGHT (866-367-5444)

Text LIGHT to 741741

Resources, education, and training

Day One

https://www.dayoneny.org/

1-800-214-4150

Confidential Hotline for help and resources

MaleSurvivor

https://www.malesurvivor.org/index.php

Support, treatment, and advocacy for male survivors of sexual abuse

Men Healing

https://menhealing.org/

Healing resources for male survivors of childhood (or adult) sexual trauma

National Association of Adult Survivors of Child Abuse (NAASCA)

http://www.naasca.org/

Child abuse trauma prevention, intervention, and recovery

National Center for PTSD

https://www.ptsd.va.gov/

Research and education on trauma and PTSD

National Child Abuse Hotline

https://www.childhelp.org/

1-800-4-A-CHILD (1-800-422-4453)

The National Domestic Violence Hotline

https://www.thehotline.org/

1-800-799-7233 or 1-800-787-3224 (TTY)

National Sexual Assault Hotline

https://www.rainn.org/

1-800-656-HOPE (4673) 24/7

Rape, abuse, and incest national network offering support groups, group therapy, individual counselors, legal aid, emergency shelter, medical attention/accompaniment, and crime victim assistance advocacy

National Suicide Prevention Lifeline

https://suicidepreventionlifeline.org/

1- 800-273-TALK (8255) 24/7

1-888-628-9454 (Spanish)

1-800-799-4889 (TTY)

Partners of Adults Sexually Abused as Children

http://www.pasac.net/

Valuable information and support for anyone in a relationship with a survivor

Safe Horizon

https://www.safehorizon.org/

1-800-621-HOPE (4673) 24/7

The nation's leading victim assistance organization, offering mental health and legal support

Sexual Trauma Services

https://www.stsm.org/

1-803-771-7273 24/7

Advocate and support system for survivors of sexual assault and abuse

Sexual Violence Center

https://www.sexualviolencecenter.org/

1-612-871-5111 24/7

Confidential services for survivors as well as their friends and family

Survivors of Incest Anonymous

https://siawso.org/

1-877-742-9761

Spiritual 12-step, self-help recovery program modeled after AA

Survivors Network of Those Abused by Priests (SNAP)

http://www.snapnetwork.org/

1-877-SNAP-HEALS (1-877-762-7432)

Largest, oldest, and most active support group for women and men wounded by religious and institutional authorities

1in6 Online Chat Line

https://1in6.org/helpline

Wealth of information and services, including a free, anonymous 24/7 helpline via online chat, plus weekly chat-based support groups for male survivors of childhood sexual abuse as well as adult sexual assault

About the Author

Veronica Crystal Young, a survivor and champion of those who have endured childhood sexual abuse, is a healthcare executive and sought-after speaker, as well as a credentialed transformational life coach and NLP practitioner. She has helped many souls release their negative hold on the past, so they can bring their talents and gifts to the world, reclaim their exceptional powers, and experience more fulfilling, meaningful lives. Veronica's background in executive and leadership training, her extensive research on childhood sexual abuse, and her own dramatic story gives her a unique insider's perspective on childhood trauma and recovery.

Veronica is also a professional actor who's worked alongside notable performers and directors, as well as starred in Broadway classic musicals such as *Cabaret, Sound of Music,* and *South Pacific.* She resides in North Hollywood and sings in the country music duo *Crystal Whiskey,* performing across Southern California. As CEO of Crystal Eyes Enterprises LLC, she is the creator and producer of the popular nature/relaxation series *TV ArtScapes®.* Visit her at veronicacrystalyoung.com.